Live First, Work Second
Getting Inside the Head of the Next Generation

Rebecca Ryan

First Printing: July 2007 by Next Generation Consulting®

Inquiries regarding permission for use of the material contained in this book should be directed to Rebecca Ryan:

> On the Web: www.nextgenerationconsulting.com
> By email: info@nextgenerationconsulting.com
> Call toll-free: 888.922.9596
> By snail mail: Next Generation Consulting
> 211 S. Paterson, Suite 100
> Madison, WI 53704

Orders: www.nextgenerationconsulting.com

ISBN 978-0-9778746-1-3

For stupid bosses everywhere, and I mean *everywhere.*

Coming Next:
People First, Profits Follow:
How Next Generation Companies™ Compete with Talent

Puppies Are Never Born in the Basket

I started listening to the next generation in 1998 when I informally interviewed[1] five of my Drake classmates at an alumni reunion. What I heard surprised me: most of them had three or four jobs in the four years since we'd been out of college. This was a serious departure from my dad's *25 years for the gold watch* ethic.

Since then, studying the next generation has grown into a business, and the interviews have grown into the tens of thousands. Each interview—like a drip of information—joins others and pools into a rich reservoir of insights, themes and trends.

I've learned that America's next generation is not going to grow up and behave more like our grandparents'. Adjusting to a *Live First, Work Second* generation is one enormous roller coaster ride. Why do we do it?

We do it because we need the next generation to work in our companies, buy our products, participate in our government, live in our cities and patronize the causes we care about. We need Next Gens to bring us booze and cigarettes when we're in the old folks' home.

We do it because we've seen how exciting work and life can be when the next generation really shows up and throws their heart into it. The Robin Hood in each of us wants to see and support more of that.

I salute you.

And I also know that, despite your best intentions and thoughtful planning, stuff happens. A new mayor is elected and forgets to jump on board the Knowledge Economy Cluetrain. Or your new boss bellows, "These young people will just have to learn to climb the corporate ladder like I did!" Or your child gets cancer and you take a leave of absence.

Life, as they say, is what happens when you're planning other things.

Face it: Puppies are never born in the basket, or on time. Your efforts to integrate *Live First* at work, in your communities, and in your organizations will get sidetracked, downplayed, and sometimes buried.

But that doesn't make the task less important, or your calling less real. When the puppies arrive—all over the carpet in the middle of the night—you deal with it and move on.

---

[1]In this context, "informal interview" means we were gathered at Peggy's, having a beer and talking.

As an entrepreneur, I have learned that the rules of business are simple:

1. Learn what the market wants;

2. Develop it; and

3. Sell it to them.

The purpose of this book is to share with you what my team and our clients have learned about the next generation so that you can develop it and sell it to them.

Let's get this party started . . . .

Rebecca Ryan

July 2007

CONTENTS

ACKNOWLEDGMENTS

"THANK YOU" is one of the most underutilized and powerful expressions in our language. Here are a couple special ones.

Thank you, Bruce Plummer, for being the first person to hire me to speak about the next generation in 1998.

Deepest thanks to my Next Generation Consulting® family: Lynn Lema, Marti, Peg Hartmann, Molly Foley, Lauren Young, and Diane Lee. And to our dedicated fans, advocates, clients, and friends. You inspire us to build better places to live and work.

Additional thanks to my extended professional family: Sandy Wight, whose editing and book experience midwifed this tome; Brody Buss, Sebastian Comella, and the team at Layer One Media, who make us look cool online; Lyn McMurray and Jim Armstrong at Good For Business, who helped us discover our purpose; Andrew Billmann and Kris Perlberg at Firepower Design, who managed the details of layout and publication; Rod Frantz, Rich Florida and the Creative Class posse, who've been unfailingly generous; and Joan Gillman, Tracy Coenen, Jack Van Rixel, Michelle Racich, Matt Hayden, and Pam Hoffman.

Although they can't read this, I want to acknowledge my dogs, Zach and Joey, who remind me to jump in the lake even when the two-leggeds scream "No!"

Weirdly, I have to thank Lawn-Boy. I got some of my best insights while mowing my yard.

Thank you, Mom and Dad. Your lives are different than mine, but the contrasts are at the heart of this book. Dad, thank you for teaching me "Five Balls" before you passed.

And to my love, Marti. You have added so much texture and quality to my life.

by Richard Florida
Author, *The Rise of the Creative Class*
and *The Flight of the Creative Class*

"Live first, work second" is a sentiment I often hear in my travels around the country and the world. Regardless of their zip codes, their native languages, or their vocations, members of the Creative Class place as much emphasis on where and how they *live* as where they work. It's a core premise of Rebecca's book, and a story that must be told.

In my experience in working with Rebecca and her team at Next Generation Consulting, I've found they are one of the most reliable sources for CEO's, mayors, legislators, economic developers, and non-profit leaders who want to attract and retain the next generation of creative workers to their communities or organizations.

In a very real way, *Live First, Work Second* helps us see our organizations and institutions through the lens of this newest crop of creatives, so that we can adjust and align in ways that will draw them in.

Let me be candid: I am a HUGE Rebecca Ryan fan.

If you've ever seen Rebecca speak, as I have, you know that she has an engaging and cutting-edge style of giving companies, communities, and economies realistic and candid advice

This is an amazing quality that has translated well to the pages of this book. This is important, because transformation is extremely difficult. But with guides like Rebecca—who bring candor and humor to the process—we can navigate and shape more relevant and engaging communities and companies for the next generation.

This book is long overdue. Rebecca's is a clear, incredibly grounded and intelligent voice in our dialogues about creativity, innovation, and community development. I know you'll find her ideas as invigorating as I have.

After you've read this book, get ready for the barnstorming tour that's sure to follow. I'm in for the ride. We need your energy, too!

—*Richard Florida*

How to read this book and use our website

While writing for you, I found myself walking a tightrope. I didn't want to insult your intelligence by overwriting what you may already know. You're smart; you get this stuff.

But I also wanted to ensure that you have the facts. I realize that some of you will use this book to slap an old-school employer upside the head in order to finally get that flex-time policy passed through HR, or to back up your case for better downtowns with your city council.

I need to provide you with the facts; I just don't want to bore you with them.

So, to keep my points brief, I've used extensive footnoting and also loaded a bunch of stuff on www.livefirstworksecond.com, which mirrors this page of our website:

www.nextgenerationconsulting.com/book

If you want to read more, you can. Please help yourself. And while you're there, share a little of what you know.

CHAPTER **1**

LIVE FIRST, WORK SECOND IN CONTEXT

1.1 *LIVE FIRST, WORK SECOND* DISCOVERED

It started over a bottle of Moose Drool™ beer.

In June 2001, I was on a three-week holiday with friends, exploring our fine national parks. We had just returned to our campsite after a long hike in Yosemite and were restoring ourselves with a cold adult beverage.

That's when Ranger Rita pulled up in her big, green ranger truck.

We silently exchanged glances. *Were we in trouble?*

Ranger Rita bounded around the truck, waving one of those pink "While You Were Out" slips. She held it towards us accusingly and seethed, "Which one of you is Rebecca Ryan?"

My heart sank.

"Come with me," she commanded. I climbed into her truck and bumped along with her in silence to the ranger station.[2]

The message was from a client. We'll call him Rich, since that's his name.

Rich was able to track me down while I was on vacation. I'm guessing this has something to do with the fact that Rich's organization does work for the Department of Defense.[3]

I called the number on the pink slip, and tried to shift mental gears from "vacation" to "work."

Rich picked up on the first ring.

"Rich!" I tried to sound cheery. "You caught me on vacation!"

Rich cut straight to business. "We just lost three of our five recruits to a competitor!"

Rich was headquartered in Baltimore. We had been working on ways to make his lab a "cooler" place to work for young physicists — flexible schedules, mentoring, the works.

---

[2] Back in high school I always wondered, *What really happens in the teacher's lounge?* I had a similar feeling when I walked into the ranger station. I wondered what the rangers actually did in there. Now I know. And I'm not telling.

[3] I share that with you in case there's any doubt that Big Brother is watching our movies, monitoring our phone calls and reading our books. (Hi there!)

"What happened?" I asked.

"They all took jobs in Denver." Rich sounded defeated. He had worked hard to make his lab a great, fun place to work for young physicists, but you could hear it in Rich's voice: his lab was in Baltimore, and he couldn't compete with Denver.

Until that moment, I had made my living helping companies become stickier places to work for young employees. And here was evidence that even a cool workplace is not enough to attract and keep young talent.

For the next 2,087 miles back home to Wisconsin, I jotted notes, wondered out loud and pestered my pals with the question, *Which is more important: a good job or a cool community?*

I was obsessed.

When I got back to the office, I tested young Americans with the same question. The result?

**Three out of four Americans under the age of 28
said a cool city is more important than a good job.**

The work/life calculus for the next generation had shifted. Their parents may have followed a job, a promotion or corporate marching orders. But the next generation was following their bliss, choosing cool cities and then finding work.

We published our findings in the *Hot Jobs-Cool Communities* report on Labor Day, 2001. On January 27, 2002, *The Wall Street Journal* published an article with the headline: "Pick a Place to Live, Then Find a Job." Later that year, *The Rise of the Creative Class* hit the best-seller list.

Economists, journalists, employers, urbanists and demographers began to notice that the next generation's ethic had shifted. They were voting with their feet and moving to places they preferred, then finding jobs.

The next generation has become very fickle about where they live and work. They want communities that "fit" their values and lifestyle. They want employers that do the same. *Live First, Work Second* is becoming the defining ethic of the next generation.

The ramifications for you, your household, your workplace and your community are broad. For starters:

- At work, keeping the next generation interested in their jobs and stimulated by their work are ongoing challenges.

- In job interviews, a new candidate asks, "I'm planning a four-week trip to Europe with my best friend. Is that allowed?" Your vacation policy for employees with less than a year of service is one week. Period.

- Your nonprofit organizations are crying for "new blood" to join their boards of directors and contribute to their causes.

- Your museums, symphonies and theaters are hosting cocktail parties before performances to lure younger patrons.

- At home, parents negotiate with their children to *get a job* instead of sitting in front of the computer, IM'ing, working on their MySpace account and texting their friends.

- Presidential politicians appear on Leno, Letterman and O'Brien to stir up interest in their campaigns.

- Newspapers spin off free weeklies to try to lure younger readers and develop new subscribers.

- Communities form Brain Drain taskforces to stem the tide of young talent flowing out their back doors.

If you recognize yourself in any of these illustrations, this book is for you. In these pages, you will see your company and your community through the lens of the next generation. In turn, you'll realize where you're missing a beat—or missing the boat—in attracting and keeping the next generation engaged.

1.2 HOW'D WE GET HERE? PUTTING *LFWS* IN CONTEXT

> *I must run a dry-cleaning shop so my sons can go to medical and law school, in order that their sons may study sociology and communications, so that their children can run vintage clothing stores, act in avant-garde theater, and work in coffee shops.*
>
> —Immigrant grandfather in Joseph Epstein's
> *Snobbery: The American Version*

If you chuckled reading this passage from Epstein's book, I'm relieved. Your response shows that at some level, you can identify with what the immigrant grandfather is expressing. Each generation builds on the next, even if they can't identify with their children's or grand-children's motives or interests.

And that's the central point of this chapter:

The next generation's *Live First, Work Second* ethic is not some out-of-nowhere, cosmic, egotistical self-expression. It's a natural next step in a generation-after-generation progression of economic life in developed societies.

Each generation wants their kids to have it better than they did. In the U.S. and other developed countries, this is actually happening. Successive generations are achieving greater prosperity for themselves and their children. And this, fair reader, is how we've arrived at a *Live First, Work Second* generation.

Let's dust off our Sociology 101 textbook; we're going to visit Uncle Abraham.

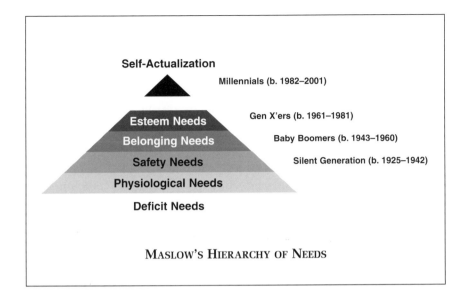

Self-Actualization

Millennials (b. 1982–2001)

Esteem Needs

Gen X'ers (b. 1961–1981)

Belonging Needs

Baby Boomers (b. 1943–1960)

Safety Needs

Silent Generation (b. 1925–1942)

Physiological Needs

Deficit Needs

MASLOW'S HIERARCHY OF NEEDS

Abraham Maslow is the scholar who gave us the *Hierarchy of Needs*.[4] I find the hierarchy especially useful in understanding each generation in its own context.

Let's take it from the bottom, shall we?

Silent Generation[5] (b. 1925-1942): Safety Needs

The Silent Generation was born and came of age during the Great Depression and WWII. President Roosevelt formed his major, enduring social policy, "The New Deal," to ensure that the Silent Generation and their successors would have adequate income to secure food, clothing and shelter. Safety needs help form the base of Maslow's Hierarchy.

As Silents' basic needs for food, shelter and clothing were secured, their children, the Baby Boomers, had the economic footing to set their sights higher up the hierarchy.

---

4 An excellent discussion of Maslow's theory is available online at http://webspace.ship.edu/cgboer/maslow.html.

5 I refer to generations as GI's, Baby Boomers, Gen X'ers, and Millennials. My reference for the birth years of each generation comes from the book *Generations* by Strauss and Howe. Go to the *Good Stuff* section at the end of this book to see a side-by-side comparison of each generation in the workplace.

Baby Boomers[6] (b. 1943-1961): Belonging Needs

Vietnam, Woodstock, ERA, the Pill, Watergate, Martin Luther King and Haight-Ashbury are all milestones along the timeline of Baby Boomers' coming of age. They're also examples of Baby Boomers' natural needs on the next "rung" of Maslow's hierarchy: the needs for affection, love, belonging and a sense of community.

Boomers marched and demonstrated, bringing millions together to secure equality for Blacks and women. The messages conveyed by Boomers' signs, songs and slogans? *All We Need Is Love, The Summer of Love,* and *Make Love, Not War.* In a Boomer world, everyone belongs.

Gen X'ers[7] (b. 1961-1981): Esteem Needs

Gen X'ers are the first generation of latchkey kids. As both of their Boomer parents headed to work—or headed off in different directions due to divorce—Gen X'ers developed heightened Esteem Needs: confidence, competence, achievement, mastery, independence and freedom.

This has translated to how Gen X'ers feel about work and society. In his book *Free Agent Nation*, Daniel Pink outlines how Gen X'ers—valuing independence and freedom—have become the first generation of job-hopping, *I rely on myself for job security* workers. Tom Peters refers to this as building "The Brand Called You."[8]

This maverick, go-it-alone mentality has had some breakout economic successes. Michael Dell (b. 1965) broke from convention and put the power to configure a computer in the hands of the consumer. Sergey Brin (b. 1973) and Larry Page (b. 1973) co-founded Google because they weren't happy with how search functions were built.

In our communities, their fierce independence makes them poor joiners of our civic and social clubs. The bowling clubs that were the rage with Baby Boomers have dwindled and died among the next generation.[9]

---

[6] Ibid.

[7] Ibid.

[8] Check out the article in the *Fast Company* magazine archives: www.fastcompany.com/online/10/brandyou.html.

[9] Dr. Robert Putnam has outlined this trend in his book, *Bowling Alone*.

Millennials[10] (b. 1982-2001): Self-Actualization Needs

Leaders often complain that our newest generation, the Millennials, are too "me-oriented." In rebuttal, consider how Millennials' "selfish actions" match those Maslow outlines as markers of self-actualization.

To self-actualize, Maslow says we should:

- **Teach people to be authentic, to be aware of their inner selves and to hear their inner-feeling voices.**

Millennials are masters at describing how they feel about work, their friends and their lives. They are learning the language of emotion at earlier and earlier ages. See the callout Hannah, the Mighty Millennial.

Hannah, the Mighty Millennial

I baby-sit other people's children as a form of birth control. (It works.) One afternoon, I was child-sitting Hannah and her one-year-old sister Maddie. Halfway through the afternoon, we had a group meltdown. Maddie began screaming and clinging to me for dear life. Hannah decided she could not live another moment without a peanut butter sandwich. As I scrambled around the kitchen gathering bread, a knife, peanut butter and a plate, Maddie became inconsolable. I put her in a headlock and proceeded to spread PB all over the kitchen. I began to growl — a low, quiet growl. Suddenly, Hannah tugged at my shorts and said, "Webecca! Stop! Bweave! Fink! Tell me what you're feeeeeewing." (Translation: "Rebecca! Stop! Breathe! Think! Tell me what you're feeeeling.")

At first, I tightened. I was not going to be coached in conflict management by a four-year-old! Then I realized:

At that moment, Hannah was the smartest person in the room. Who says the oldest or most experienced person has the best ideas? In this case, I learned a valuable lesson — to express my feelings — taught by a Mighty Millennial.

---

[10] I refer to generations as GI's, Baby Boomers, Gen X'ers, and Millennials. My reference for the birth years of each generation comes from the book Generations by Strauss and Howe. Go to the Good Stuff section at the end of this book to see a side-by-side comparison of each generation in the workplace.

- **Teach people to transcend their cultural conditioning and become world citizens.**

Millennials have taken service-learning trips all over the world. Many are bilingual and take up studies in global business and global marketing, and are giving years of their lives to global service opportunities.

- **We should help people discover their vocations in life, their callings, fates or destinies. This is especially focused on finding the right career and the right mate.**

Millennials are waiting longer to get married, and they have more career angst than previous generations. They want to make sure they're choosing the right partner or career. Before choosing anything—a new gizmo, a class or a profession—they research voraciously on various websites like epinions, vault.com and ratemyprofessors.com.

- **We should refresh consciousness, teaching people to appreciate beauty and the other good things in nature and in life.**

Millennials take time off—vacation or sabbaticals—to travel, explore and experience. They're not waiting until retirement to drink fine wines, choose good restaurants and invest in brands that have excellent aesthetics and design.

- **We should teach people to transcend trifling problems and grapple with life's serious problems. These include injustice, pain, suffering and death.**

Millennials ask in job interviews about an employer's philanthropic efforts, paid time off policy for community service, and commitment to the environment. They want to work for a company whose values match theirs, and they want their companies to adhere to the Google mantra, "Do no evil."

Humpty Dumpty Has Fallen... and the Next Generation Can Put It Back Together Again

American institutions—politics, marriage, religion, civic life—are crumbling because they were built on assumptions that are no longer valid. Designed to work in a society of smokestacks and factories, today's institutions are facing a shelf life shortened by the real-time, just-in-time demands of a Knowledge Economy.

Let's play a little game. You name an institution and I'll provide some evidence that it's crumbling and how the next generation is already working to repair it.

Ready? Here we go.

You say, "Politics."

I say, "Don't make it so easy for me to make my point." More people believe scientists than they do politicians. Voter knowledge on core political subjects is stupefying. If a vital democracy is based on an informed public, this institution is in deep doo-doo.

How the Next Generation adapts: Moveon.org showed that voters can mobilize for change *and* that the polls can be affected. Political blogs and online petition-signing are just two ways that political energy is being captured and spread.

What are the results? Voting among 18- to 24-year-olds surged by 11 percentage points in 2004 . . . this, after sliding 16 percentage points in the presidential election years between 1972 and 2000.

You say, "Education."

Let's see: The K–12 education calendar was designed around an agrarian planting and harvesting schedule that hasn't applied to most of our school-aged children since before Jed Clampett discovered oil. We've known for awhile that year-round school is better for kids' learning. Meanwhile, our kids fall farther behind in math and science, the very subjects on which tomorrow's economy is being built.

How the Next Gen adapts: The IQ Academy and Malcolm Shabazz City High School in Madison, WI, demonstrate that alternatives to traditional classroom learning work well in transferring knowledge to children of all backgrounds. In Philadelphia, a high-tech high school opened its doors in October 2006 without books. No paper and no pencils, either. Just laptops . . . standard issue.[11]

You say, "Religion." I give you the Catholic church's priest scandal.

How the Next Gen adapts: Megachurches have capitalized on

---

[11] For the whole story, visit www.npr.org/templates/story/story.php?storyId=6210622.

Americans' growing demand for spiritual connection. Forget incense and organs. Megachurches use live bands, multimedia technology and jean-clad pastors to appeal to those seeking spiritual footing.

You say, "Rotary." I point to *Bowling Alone*, which shows that Rotary, Kiwanis, Elks, Moose and other Large Game-Named Organizations are in decline. Those civic institutions were invented at or near the turn of the century, when the economy was aflutter with industrialization. As people moved to cities with better economic opportunity, they needed new venues to connect with each other and to do what all of us want to do: leave our communities better places than we found them.

How the next gen adapts: Rotary's Next Gens are skipping lunch and starting their own Young Professionals Organizations. They're tech-enabled, offer real-time get-togethers and help young professionals plug into the community.

In September '06, 135 leaders of YPOs were in Madison, WI to share ideas on how to further engage the next generation of civic and community leaders. Their results are astonishing. They're rewiring school districts, helping companies relocate great talent and giving each other a reason to believe in the future of the community. Many Chambers of Commerce have added YPO leaders to their boards, and with full voting rights.

You. What does the future hold for you?

You don't have to be a member of the next generation to hold a *Live First, Work Second* ethic or to participate in your life, your work and society in new ways. Ask yourself, "Does the way I work, participate, vote, connect and recreate still work for me, my family and my lifestyle?" If not, alternatives are being invented as you read this. Don't feel guilty for realizing that something's not working.

Something's not working for a lot of us, because nearly everything is changing.

You'd never try to wear the pants you wore in high school. Your body is different and the styles have changed. The same is true in the rest of your life.

So you see, the *Live First* generation is right on time. In their book, *The Fourth Turning*, Strauss and Howe suggest that all cultures go through four eras, or turnings (see illustration). The institutional collapse currently occurring is right on time, and the next generations—the pragmatic Gen X'ers and the idealistic Millennials—are just the remedy we need.

The four turnings, with examples from recent U.S. history are:

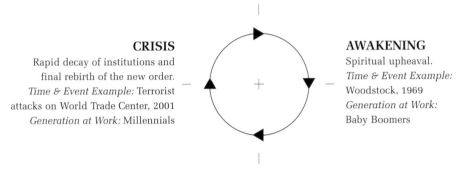

HIGH
Institutions strengthen, and a new civic order emerges.
Time & Event Example: New Deal of the 1930s
Generation at Work: Traditionalists

CRISIS
Rapid decay of institutions and
final rebirth of the new order.
Time & Event Example: Terrorist
attacks on World Trade Center, 2001
Generation at Work: Millennials

AWAKENING
Spiritual upheaval.
Time & Event Example:
Woodstock, 1969
Generation at Work:
Baby Boomers

UNRAVELING
Institutions weaken, individuals strengthen, the civic order
begins to decay and a new value system begins to unfold.
Time & Event Example: Iran-Contra Scandal, 1983-88
Generation at Work: Gen X'ers

Our institutions are in crisis because they were designed to meet society's needs in a time of smokestacks and factories. To survive, our institutions—and all of us—must get with the times and learn to adapt to a flat world, Google and MySpace. This evolution is natural, and—at least from my perch—exciting. And the *Live First* generation is exactly what we need to rebuild these institutions for contemporary times.

Go to the ***Good Stuff*** section at the end of the book for:

- A side-by-side comparison of the four primary generations living in the U.S. today

- A short reading on the four S's of Generation X (b. 1961–1981)

- A short reading on the four S's of the Millennials (b. 1982–2001)

1.3 IT AIN'T OVER YET: FOUR EXACERBATING TRENDS

In the last chapter, we talked about how we got here—how *Live First, Work Second* has become the guiding ethic of the next generation.

But it ain't over yet. There are four trends that will amplify the *Live First* impact on our companies, our communities and our society.

Each of these trends has been written about extensively in other books. So, to save your eyes—not to mention our trees—I've limited my remarks to the most salient points. The *Good Stuff* section at the back of this book has more resources on each of these trends.

Trend 1: From an Economy of Goods to a Knowledge Economy

To understand the drama of a shifting economy, I want to share a personal story.

Dad and Me

My parents are members of the "Silent Generation." My dad was born in 1925; my mom, in '26. After Dad completed seventh grade, he went to work on the family farm straddling Abbotsford and Dorchester, Wisconsin. Drafted at age 18 to serve in World War II, he completed boot camp in Arkansas and eventually was shipped off to Italy.[12] Dad was Private First Class 36847644. (Dad kept that number in his head. I keep it in my contact management system.)

Lucky for Dad, the war ended just before he was sent up to the front lines, but not before many in his troupe were wounded or killed. He was advised by his commanding officers not to get too close to his fellow PFCs. Losing a friend could get in the way of fighting a war.

When he returned to Wisconsin, Dad worked for a while on the family farm, which by that time had moved west to Montana. After Dad and Mom married in 1952, they moved to West Bend, Wisconsin—in large part, because the West Bend Company was employing thousands to make aluminum pots and pans. In 1956, Dad buttoned up his blue-

---

[12] Information provided in letters from my mother, Inez Schwoch, in 2004 and 2005.

collared work shirt with "Elmer" embroidered in yellow, white and black on the upper-left chest and started work for the West Bend Company.

There's nothing like a war to ignite an industrial economy, and World War II was no exception. By the 1950s, the manufacturing economy (an "Economy of Goods") was revving along, carrying families into a period of relative affluence.

My family was a beneficiary. Mom and Dad built a 2,000-square-foot ranch home at 624 Cabrini Circle, complete with three bedrooms, three baths and the ugliest kitchen carpet you've ever seen. The best part of our house was its large, unfinished basement, where my brother, my friends and I would retreat to roller skate, play Ping Pong or shoot pool when it was too dark or too humid outside.

Of the 14 families who lived on Cabrini Circle while we did, eight had heads of households who worked in the Manufacturing Economy. Three more worked as public servants for the postal service or the police department, and the rest were white-collar workers in management or professional services.

By the time Dad took early retirement in 1989, he had invested 33 years at the West Bend Company. My brother and I were raised our entire lives in one city. Dad received a gold watch on his 25th anniversary at the West Bend Company. At his retirement party, he was given an aluminum saucepan, an icon of the West Bend Company's rise to manufacturing greatness. On the base of the pan, a clock was mounted. It runs on a couple of double-A's. In the center of the clock is a placard that reads:

Elmer Schwoch
33 Years of Service

Dad's pot-clock still hangs shrine-like in my parents' dining room.

At its peak, the West Bend Company employed 1,500 workers. Today, its legacy organization, West Bend Housewares, employs 40.[13] In my dad's lifetime, the West Bend Company was bought and sold by Dart Industries, Dart & Kraft, Premak International, Illinois Tool Works, and Regal Ware, Inc.

Fast-forward to today. My dad's daughter (that's me) makes her living with a MacBook, a small team of MBAs with white-collar backgrounds, a few choice Web-based survey and mapping tools, and a select suite of project, design and multimedia software programs.

In Dad's lifetime, the U.S. economy shifted from an Economy of Goods to a Knowledge Economy. Dad worked primarily with his hands. I work primarily with my head. The differences between Dad's Economy and My Economy are outlined below:

	Dad's Economy: **Economy of Goods**	My Economy: **Knowledge Economy**
What's needed for economic self-sufficiency	Strong back Good alarm clock	Education and training Constant upgrading of skills
Work ethic	Heads down, butts up	Work smarter, not harder Live first, work second
Decision-making mantra	"Do what you're told."	Take initiative
Where you live	Company town	Cool Community
Where your co-workers live	In your area code	Anywhere on earth
Where you work	Factory or plant	Everywhere, even on vacation
Regular meetings	Face-to-face	Teleconference or videoconference
Work hierarchy	Top-down, bureaucratic	Flat; everyone's a decision-maker

To put the economic shift from Dad's Economy to My Economy in more quantitative financial terms, consider the biggest names of Dad's Economy: Boeing, Ford, General Motors and Lockheed Martin. Here are their respective market capitalizations:

---

[13] From an email interview with Phyllis Schaefer, West Bend Housewares LLC.

Company	(TICKER):	$ Market Capitalization (in Billions)
Boeing	(BA):	$67.55B
Ford Motor Company	(F):	$15.90B
General Motors	(GM):	$18.63B
Lockheed Martin	(LMT):	$40.98B
Subtotal:		$143.06B

Together, these companies have a combined market capitalizations of $143.06 billion. This is far less than Google's market capitalization:

Google (GOOG): $151.80B

Did you "Google" today? Of course you did. You may even have the Google toolbar installed on your Web browser. You may be an Ego-Googler.[14]

You may be using Google Maps or Gmail. You may have visited your childhood neighborhood with Google Earth.

What does Google manufacture?

Nothing. Google doesn't "make" anything. Google invents algorithms to help you find obscure information in the fastest, most accurate way. Google manufactures nothing, yet its market capitalization is greater than the greatest brands of my dad's economy.

Yes, Virginia, the economy has shifted.

And central to a Knowledge Economy are Knowledge Workers.

Trend 2: Fewer Younger Workers

Peter Drucker originally coined the term "knowledge worker" in his 1959 book, *Landmarks of Tomorrow*. Drucker said that knowledge workers include *anyone who works for a living at the tasks of developing or using knowledge.*[15]

Sounds like darn near everyone I know.

Knowledge workers are critical because they create market value. In our Google example, the company's value is in its algorithms, which pours out of the heads of its talent. By some estimates, knowledge workers' "intangible assets" now account for around 70 percent of the

---

[14] Ego-Google: [Verb] To type one's own name into the Google search tool in an effort to learn one's ranking(s).

[15] http://searchcrm.techtarget.com/sDefinition/0,,sid11_gci212450,00.html.

Fortune 500's value. In my dad's economy, it was about 20 percent.[16]

There are going to be fewer of them to go around in the coming years. Some call this talent shortage a "Silent Crisis." Peter Drucker calls it the number-one issue facing us:

> *In the developed countries, the dominant factor in the Next Society will be something to which most people are only just beginning to pay attention: the rapid growth in the older population and the rapid shrinking of the younger generation.*
>
> — Peter Drucker, *Managing in the Next Society*

Drucker was talking about demographics, the Mother of All Trends. Demographics are shorthand for population statistics, and the world is facing some prescient realities:

- The birth rates—even in China[17] and Brazil—are well below the replacement rate of 2.2 births per household.

- One in four Europeans is over the age of 65.[18]

- By 2010, about 64 million workers—40 percent of the United States workforce—will be poised for retirement, though not all will choose to leave.[19]

- By 2010, the number of people ages 35 to 44 in the nation's workforce will decline by 10 percent.[20]

- By 2010, the number of workers ages 45 to 54 will grow by 21 percent, and the number of 55- to 64-year-olds will grow by 52 percent.[21] (See chart on following page.)

---

[16] Adrian Woolridge, "The Battle for Brainpower," *The Economist*, October 7, 2006, p.4.

[17] How can China—a land of 1,313,973,713 (July '06 estimate)—have a talent shortage? Remember the "one child" policy of family planning?

[18] "Top Ten Trends" from Now and Next, www.nowandnext.com/?action=top_trend/list_trends&sectorId=1.

[19] Lynne Morton, "Managing the Mature Workforce," (Report #1369), published by The Conference Board, available at www.conference-board.org/publications/describe.cfm?id=1007.

[20] Ibid.

[21] Ibid.

- By 2025, the number of people ages 15 to 64 is projected to fall 7 percent in Germany, 9 percent in Italy and 14 percent in Japan.[22]

- America's 500 largest companies are expected to lose half of their senior managers in the next five years or so. Civil service attrition is expected to be even higher.[23]

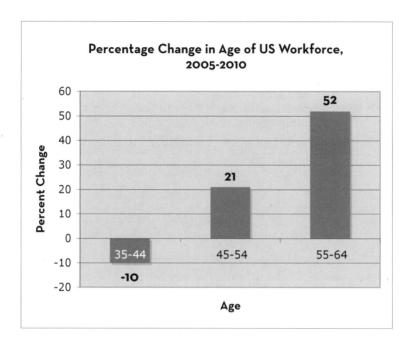

Percentage Change in Age of US Workforce, 2005-2010

Implications: *What Does This Trend Mean to You?*

As the population ages, several things happen:

1. There's a smaller pool of new employees to replace Baby Boomers, so the supply of talent is shrinking, and the battle for talent heats up.

2. The balance of power shifts to employees, who will demand more *Live First, Work Second* benefits like flex-time, compressed workweeks, telecommuting and more paid time off.

---

[22] Adrian Woolridge, The Battle for Brainpower, *The Economist*, October 7, 2006, p. 4.
[23] Ibid.

3. There's an experience gap; new workers cannot make up for the institutional knowledge and experience of retiring workers.

4. As Baby Boomers retire, they create new demands for services.

These trends will put stress on every institution: the workplace, non-profit organizations, the arts, Social Security, health care, government, etc. If you're not already doing so, you'll soon be competing neck-and-neck with other organizations that will beg, borrow and poach from you, dipping into an ever-smaller pool of workers, board members, patrons, volunteers, donors, taxpayers and citizens. Some of your organizations will fold or die when this economic reality becomes clear:

A smaller generation cannot feed all the organizational appetites created by the Baby Boom.

Knowledge Workers or the Creative Class?
Fuel for the Knowledge Economy

In a lecture to a bunch of smarties at the John F. Kennedy School of Government at Harvard University in May 1995,[24] Peter Drucker announced:

"Knowledge workers, even though only a large minority of the work-force, already give the emerging knowledge society its character, its leadership, its central challenges and its social profile. They may not be the ruling class of the knowledge society, but they already are its leading class. In their characteristics, their social positions, their values and their expectations, they differ fundamentally from any group in history that has ever occupied the leading, let alone the dominant, position."

In 2002, Richard Florida wrote a best-selling book, *The Rise of the Creative Class*. In it, Dr. Florida divides the Creative Class into two

---

[24] To read the full transcript of this lecture, go to
www.ksg.harvard.edu/ifactory/ksgpress/www/ksg_news/transcripts/drucklec.htm.

subgroups: the "Super Creative Core" and the broader Creative Class. The Creative Class is an extension of Peter Drucker's earlier definition of Knowledge Workers, updated for contemporary job descriptions.

Dr. Florida writes:

"I define the core of the Creative Class to include people in science and engineering, architecture and design, education, arts, music and entertainment, whose economic function is to create new ideas, new technology and/or new creative content. Around the core, the Creative Class also includes a broader group of creative professionals in business and finance, law, health care and related fields. These people engage in complex problem-solving that involves a great deal of independent judgment and requires high levels of education or human capital. In addition, all members of the Creative Class — whether they are artists or engineers, musicians or computer scientists, writers or entrepreneurs — share a common creative ethos that values creativity, individuality, difference, and merit."[25]

In other words, the Creative Class includes all of Drucker's knowledge workers, plus actors, musicians and Will Smith, who does a little bit of all of it. Florida contends that the Creative Class comprises 30 percent of the entire workforce and generates more than half of all wages and economic impact.

Both Drucker's and Florida's definitions classify the workers who generate and manage information and content. Both authors agree that their respective classes command a leading, influential economic and social position in a changing world.

Implications: *What Does This Trend Mean to You?*

The rewards of the Knowledge Economy will go to knowledge workers and the innovative companies that unleash their talents.

---

[25] Richard Florida, *The Rise of the Creative Class*, p. 8.

Are you working in the Knowledge Economy?

Using the following scale, rank yourself, your coworkers and your workplace based on these statements.

SCALE
1 – Absolutely describes me and/or my workplace.
2 – Sort of describes me and/or my workplace.
3 – Doesn't really describe me and/or my workplace.
4 – Doesn't describe me and/or my workplace at all.

____ I am expected to learn and grow through training and "stretch" experiences at work.

____ I am encouraged to use my creativity and problem-solving skills at work.

____ My supervisor emphasizes a culture where co-workers share information and knowledge.

____ My manager or organization rewards people who create better ways to do things.

____ I work with people who are as smart, or smarter, than I am.

____ Our company "never settles" and is constantly working to do things better, more efficiently or with greater innovation.

____ My organization is considered an innovation leader in our industry by our peers.

____ **TOTAL SCORE**

SCORING

7–15: Congratulations! You and your company are well-positioned to compete in the Knowledge Economy.

16–24: It may be time for you, your team and/or your organization to take a hard look at the most innovative organizations in your industry and determine a plan to differentiate yourselves from them and compete with them.

25–32: Uh-oh. Your company's best days may have already happened. You and/or your organization might be on a crash course to irrelevance. Upgrade your skills and/or challenge your organization to become more innovative . . . pronto!

Trend 3: Knowledge Economy *Everywhere*

In a Knowledge Economy, any place—and I mean *any place*—that can attract or develop and retain Knowledge Workers has a fighting chance. Estonia, for example, currently has a higher concentration of the "Creative Class" than the U.S.

How fluent are you in the global Knowledge Economy? Try this: Match the high-tech region in Column A to the city and country in Column B and a key employer or brainiac in Column C.

Column A	Column B	Column C
Electronics City	Bangalore, India	Infosys
Biopolis	Singapore	Dr. Alan Colman[26]
Research Triangle	Chapel Hill, USA	IBM
Silicon Valley	San Jose, CA	Cisco Systems

The solution? Draw a straight, horizontal line across each of the rows. Grab your psychic passports. We're going for a ride!

---

[26] Dr. Colman was on the research team that cloned Dolly the Sheep.

Biopolis will eat your genetically modified lunch.

Since its launch, Biopolis has attracted Dr. Alan Colman, Dr. Edison Liu,[27] and the entire genomics department from Kyoto University. Of the 4,000 Ph.D.s who call Singapore home, over one-fourth are ex-pats from other countries.

Seems Singapore is serious about becoming the biotech capital of the universe.

So, how are they doing it? They're putting their money where their aspirations are. To attract big brains, Singapore made it easy for top researchers and scientists to exercise their big, fat craniums.

Singapore provides research funding and state-of-the-art lab space—free. Compare that to the U.S., where researchers must write grants, wait hat-in-hand for funding and fight for labs.

In return for its generous financial support of their research, Singapore asks its biotech immigrants to spend some quality time attracting others. Voila! A built- in recruiting team.

In the words of Lee Kuan Yew, Singapore's elder statesman, "Trained talent is the yeast that transforms a society and makes it rise."

Government agencies are in lockstep alignment and are providing excellent service to help Singapore kick bio-booty. Singapore's Ministry of Manpower (MOM) is putting on a full-court press to attract talent and make it seamless to immigrate. Only 3 percent of companies experience difficulty with the Singapore immigration authorities, compared to 24 percent in China and 46 percent in the United States.[28]

Electronics City

Bangalore is India's software capital, home to more than 140,000 software engineers—more than Silicon Valley. India's National Association of Software and Service Companies (NASSCOM) calculates that India has 28 percent of the world's IT offshore talent.[29]

Indian workers are diligent, English-speaking and cheap. The wages of an Indian graduate are roughly 12 percent that of an American grad.

---

[27] Dr. Liu was the top U.S. cancer researcher before accepting his current position as Executive Director of the Genome Institute of Singapore; www.ori.nus.edu.sg/pibios_edisonliu.html.

[28] Woolridge, p. 13.

[29] Adrian Woolridge, "The world is our oyster," *The Economist*, October 7, 2006, p. 9.

Indian graduates work an average of 2,350 hours a year, compared with 1,900 hours in America and 1,700 in Germany.[30]

Singapore and India demonstrate that the spoils of economic abundance are no longer reserved for a handful of elite countries. Iceland, Vietnam, Estonia, China and other countries are not only developing, they're leapfrogging their competitors, thanks to their progressive investments in human and venture capital:

- From 1986 to 2001, China, Taiwan, South Korea and Japan awarded more doctoral degrees in science and engineering than the United States.

- Between 1991 and 2003, research and development spending in America trailed that of China, Singapore, South Korea and Taiwan.

- From 1991 to 2003, China out-invested the United States by a billion dollars.[31]

Implications: *What Does This Trend Mean to You?*

The 20th Century was the American Century. Industrialization and the Economy of Goods smiled on us. In the 21st Century, we're already a kilometer[32] behind. The Knowledge Economy has gone global, and the United States—through its foreign policy, economic priorities and *let's celebrate the good old days* farm-subsidy legislation—is flat-footed in response.

Want to be a player in a global Knowledge Economy? Here are three things you can do:

1. **Write to your elected officials.**[33] Demand that earmarks be eliminated so that true national priorities—especially educating all of our kids to be Knowledge Workers and committing a greater share of resources to R&D—become a focus of our investments.

---

[30] Ibid.

[31] Timothy O'Brien, "Not Invented Here," *New York Times*, November 13, 2005.

[32] And that's another thing: Why didn't the U.S. adopt metric when the rest of the world did?

[33] Search by zip code for your Congressperson at www.congress.org/congressorg/home/.

2. **Educate yourself**. If you have a high school degree, get a technical degree. If you have an associate's degree, go for your bachelor's degree. If you have your bachelor's, consider getting professional certification in your field, going on for a master's degree, or enrolling in management or executive education seminars. It's called the "Knowledge Economy" for a reason: Knowledge *is* power. And to compete, you must constantly upgrade your skills and abilities.

3. **Travel**. If you really want to understand the global economy, get out of your own country. Travel to China, Singapore, Dubai or any other emerging economy. Their infrastructures are state-of-the-art, they are completely wired, and they're leapfrogging the merchants of the industrial economy.

Trend 4: New Leadership Needed

Leadership. What a loaded word! We complain that we lack leadership, but we keep electing, heralding and reading about leaders who, in my opinion, don't reflect the sensibilities of the *Live First, Work Second* generation.

Maybe we just don't know what we want. The economy has shifted. Our institutions are showing signs of age. We need leaders, yes. We also need an updated definition of *leadership*, because the "leaders" of my dad's generation—public officials and captains of industry—have lost their luster.

Need proof? Let's look at a sample of our top leaders—U.S. presidents—through the lens of the next generation.[34]

President Nixon, the first president most Gen X'ers remember, resigned the office over something to do with a little wiretapping scheme called Watergate.

President Reagan proclaimed in November 1986, "We did not—repeat, did not—trade weapons or anything else for hostages, nor will we." Four months later—on March 4, 1987—Reagan admitted in a televised national address, "A few months ago, I told the American people I did not trade arms for hostages. My heart and my best intentions still

---

[34] From the Mendacity Index, Washington Monthly, March 2003. Full text available at www.washingtonmonthly.com/features/2003/0309.mendacity-index.html.

tell me that's true, but the facts and the evidence tell me it is not." Reagan also said that although the Iran-Contra scandal happened on his watch, he had no knowledge of it.[35]

In 1988, **President George H.W. Bush** said, "Read my lips: No new taxes." In his budget for 1991, Bush raised the top income tax rate and boosted levies on gasoline, tobacco and booze.

During a press conference on January 26, 1998, **President Clinton** declared, "I did not have sexual relations with that woman, Miss Lewinsky." Clinton later admitted that he had indeed received oral sex from Miss Lewinsky, a White House intern at the time. (Raise your hand if you don't think sexual relations includes oral sex.)

In making the case for a U.S. invasion of Iraq, **President George W. Bush** stated in early 2003, "The British government has learned that Saddam Hussein recently sought significant quantities of uranium from Africa." Yet the CIA had itself previously warned top White House officials and British Intelligence that the reports of an Iraqi attempt to buy uranium from African countries were almost certainly untrue, and no nuclear program or weapons of mass destruction were then found, or have yet to be found, in Iraq.

Republic of Doubt

To be a leader, you have to be trusted. That much has not changed. But today's leaders can't be trusted. The benevolent captains of industry who guided my dad's economy were replaced by greedy bastards who make up to 400 times as much as the average worker, and further pad their bottom lines through lies, corruption and outright evasion. Enron, WorldCom and Global Crossing are illustrations #1, #2, and #3.

---

[35] I wrote a 20-page, 8th-grade research paper on the Iran-Contra scandal.

Americans are living in a "Republic of Doubt."

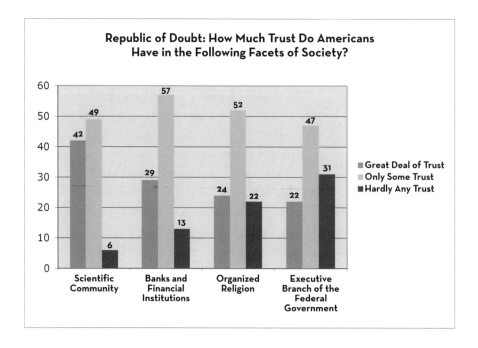

Source: National Opinion Research Center, University of Chicago interviews conducted August 2004–January 2005. Sample: 2,812 adults.

When scientists replace leaders of banks, religions, and Presidents as people whom Americans trust most, something treacherous is afoot. It's not that scientists shouldn't be trusted. The larger issue is that the leaders who harbor our money, direct our faith, and lead our country are *less trusted*.

Trust, Information & Transparency

Perhaps trust was easier to earn when information wasn't as widely shared. Ignorance, as they say, is bliss. Let me share a personal story.

For my parents' generation (Silent Generation, b. 1925-1940), what the doctor said was taken as The Word of The Lord. They just don't question their doctor. They take their medicine . . . quietly. This is, after all, the Silent Generation.

When my dad was diagnosed with cancer, I—a Gen X'er motivated by the confidence that information brings—jumped online to learn all about his disease. I went with my parents to Dad's appointments. There, I took pages of notes and asked gobs of questions. My parents were appalled.

After four years, Dad's treatments weren't working. Dr. V made her final recommendation: a targeted drug therapy. It was a last-ditch effort. Results could not be predicted because the drug was new and Dad's body was tired.

A day later, I read about the drug Dr. V had recommended in *The Wall Street Journal*. It came with a price tag of $13,000 per treatment. Dr. V hadn't mentioned this to my parents, but cost wouldn't really be a concern to my parents, since Medicare was picking up much of the tab. I called my parents that night to tell them about the article I'd read.

The next week, my dad informed Dr. V that he was not going to proceed with the therapy. He couldn't justify the cost, especially since it couldn't guarantee remission. In effect, my dad was done fighting. Like a good soldier, he was calling an end to it.

In hindsight, I wonder if telling my parents about the price tag was a piece of information they didn't need to know.

And there's the rub. I was raised in an information society. For my generation, having and sharing information is part of our predisposition. My dad was raised in a "don't ask, don't tell" culture, where you trusted your leaders, doctors and presidents. Sometimes, it was better *not* to know.

No wonder my Dad trusted his presidents, and I don't.

Like it or not, we are living in a Knowledge Economy, loaded with information. *The New York Times* Sunday edition contains more information than the average 18th Century citizen saw in a lifetime.[36]

Our ability to access, gather, analyze and manipulate information is central to our economic lives and, if you ask me, to ordering take-out.

But with all this information swirling about, we need different skills from our leaders.

- We need leaders who are information-savvy, who can sort through a flurry of data and spot the trends.

- We need leaders who have the ability to co-lead and delegate well. In a Knowledge Economy, we need multiple, well-trained

---

[36] Teresa and Chuck Easler, *The Power to Connect*, published by Corporate Vision, 2004, p. 14.

sets of eyes and ears to steer the course. There's a reason that air traffic-control towers have multiple controllers.

- We need leaders who can communicate a complex or difficult issue in a simple, clear way.

- We need leaders who are comfortable working and leading in a networked, decentralized decision-making grid, where they will not always be the smartest person—or provide the last word.

Beetle Bailey goes AWOL

Perhaps the best illustration of the tension between my dad's leadership style (top-down, command-and-control) and the leadership required in a Knowledge Economy is being played out in our U.S. military.

The U.S. military invented top-down, command-and-control leadership. My dad learned this style firsthand during his time as a Private First Class in the U.S. Army. He understood "marching orders" and "rank-and-file." I call this Beetle Bailey Management[37] after my dad's favorite cartoon. And it worked.

Wars were won. The Great Depression ended. Wall Street was established. It was the advent of the Great Society in which America's burgeoning middle class boomed.

But then the economy shifted. A new kind of "war" started, one based on the exchange of information and access to technology. And our leaders had no precedent for how to fight it.

The solution? Replace Beetle Bailey Management with a new kind of training. And that's exactly what the military did. Today, the U.S. military uses video games to train next-generation soldiers. One game in particular, *Think Like a Commander*, teaches soldiers that everyone's a general. The game's goal is to train soldiers in a decentralized, networked model of warfare in which even the lowest-ranking officer can call in an air strike or a tank battalion.[38]

---

[37] I use the term "Beetle Bailey Management" to describe top-down, command-and-control management as characterized in the cartoon by the same name, whose characters included Sergeant Snorkel, General Halftrack, Lieutenant Cosmo, Otto the Dog, and Privates Rocky and Zero, among others. Beetle Bailey was one of my Dad's favorite cartoons and one of the ways I came to understand his world view . . . and his sense of humor.

[38] To read the full story, go to www.wired.com/wired/archive/12.09/warroom.html.

The military is abandoning its top-down, command-and-control management style in favor of a decentralized model. That's like David Letterman giving up Paul Shaffer . . . or Drew Carey giving up those damn glasses. The same institution that invented Beetle Bailey Management is now abandoning it, because Beetle Bailey Management can't compete in a war taking place in the Knowledge Economy.

After the September 11, 2001, terrorist attacks, my dad compared the War on Terror to World War II.

"You know," Dad said, "it was easier in my war. You just shot at the guy with the different-colored uniform. Today, you don't know who the enemy is."

Dad's insight perfectly explains the military's rationale for abandoning the Beetle Bailey Management model: the generals fighting the war can't tell whom they're fighting. Their best hope is to arm everyone—especially those on the front lines—with training, knowledge and skills, and then trust them to use force in the right situations. This is an excellent example of the new kind of leadership needed in a Knowledge Economy. Here's another example:

Winning a Nobel Peace Prize
In 1997, Jody Williams shared the Nobel Peace Prize with the International Campaign to Ban Landmines (ICBL) for her efforts to eradicate landmines. In the end, she got signatures from leaders of 120 countries.[39]

When reporters swarmed her home in Vermont the day of the Peace Prize announcement, Ms. Williams was asked, "How'd you do it?"

"Email," she responded.

From 1991 to 1997, ICBL leveraged cyberspace to mobilize ten dozen countries to sign the ban. Sometimes Ms. Williams would be up by 3:30 a.m. to send email updates around the globe.[40]

Implications: *What Does This Trend Mean to You?*
Now, more than ever, America needs leaders who understand that power is not to be controlled and centralized. It is to be shared, developed

---

[39] In another display of global leadership, the United States was not among the ICBL's signators.
[40] To read more about how email is being leveraged by the ICBL, go to
www.cnn.com/SPECIALS/1997/nobel.prize/stories/internet.coalition/.

and put to productive use. In the words of Margaret Mead, a leader is anyone who wants to help.

Are you a leader?[41] Are you capable and ready to lead in a Knowledge Economy?

Take the quiz below, total your points and find out:

	1 YES! This totally describes me.	2 This sort of describes me.	3 This doesn't really describe me	4 Aaack! This is not me AT ALL.
This week at work, I asked for, and considered, other people's opinions before making a decision.				
I usually work collaboratively with a team of people to manage and lead projects.				
I can motivate and engage all kinds of people, regardless of their backgrounds, work experience or seniority.				
I'm committed to building a high-performance team, regardless of my own rewards and recognition.				
I admit when I'm wrong.				
I balance data and information with instinct and experience when making key decisions.				
People whom I respect gravitate towards me and ask for my input and counsel.				
Subtotals for each column:				
Grand Total:				

41 Young professionals with leadership skills should make sure they're connecting with their local YP organization. See www.ypcommons.org.

SCORING

7–10: Wowee!! Even if you don't have a fancy title at work, you're probably considered a leader by your peers.

11–16: You definitely have what it takes to be a leader for the next generation. I hope you're using your leadership skills at work and in your community.

16–24: Either you're stuck in a command-and-control mindset or in a top-down workplace. If you find yourself having a hard time working with the next generation, now you know why.

Trends & Implications *At A Glance*

Exacerbating Trend	Implication
1. From an Economy of Goods to a Knowledge Economy	To garner their knowledge and productivity, employers will have to create *Live First* value propositions that honor the next generation's desire to spend time with their families, lead balanced lives, have time off and find personal fulfillment.
2. Fewer younger workers	Increasing competition for young workers/citizens/board members/volunteers/patrons will force organizations to cater to the next generation's *Live First* ethic.
3. Knowledge Economy *everywhere*	Cities will have increasing pressure from companies to invest in community infrastructure to lure and keep talent. Talent will migrate globally to the best communities, and companies will follow talent.
4. New leadership needed	New leadership styles will be needed to engage the next generation of knowledge workers. Meetup.org, MySpace.com and YouTube are already demonstrating the power of decentralized, networked affiliations.

CHAPTER 2

COOL COMMUNITIES: TALENT MAGNETS FOR THE *LIVE FIRST* GENERATION

2.1 COOL COMMUNITIES: THREE TRUTHS AND A LIE

Have you ever played the game, "Three Truths and a Lie?" The goal is to share four things about yourself, including one that's false. Your co-players have to guess which of your disclosures is a lie.

If your co-players know you well, they'll be able to sniff out the lie. Alternatively, if you're a terrible liar, you make it easy for them to guess.

Let's play a quick round.

Here are four things about me. Which one is a lie?

- I started next generation Consulting on April Fool's Day, 1998.

- I played professional basketball in Budapest, Hungary.

- I baby-sit other people's children as a form of birth control.

- I'm 6 feet 1 inch tall.

Which one is the lie?

The first one is true. I started Next Generation Consulting on April Fool's Day—without a business plan. Hence, the fool.

I also tried out—and made the cut—for a professional basketball team during my junior year of college, while I was studying at Közgáz University in Budapest, Hungary.[42] In fact, one of my team photos is on the next page.

I also baby-sit other people's children as a form of birth control. It works.

The last one is false: I'm only 6 feet tall.

My point? *The difference between a truth and a lie is sometimes a matter of an inch.* If you want to attract and keep the *Live First, Work*

---

[42] I tried out for the team because a friend double-dog dared me. I usually accept double-dog dares, because my inner tomboy-girl talks smack to me if I don't.

Second generation to your community, then you need to examine the truths—and the lies—that are swirling in your communities. Sometimes the difference between them is minute, and that teeny, tiny variance can make all the difference in your long-term results.

That's me in the back row, first from the left.

Three Truths and a Lie in Your Community

Truth #1: ***The Knowledge Economy doesn't play by the old rules of economic development.***

If you've attended an economic development conference lately, you've probably noticed that they are full—and I mean *full*—of the Pale, Male and Stale (PMS). You don't have to be white, a man or hovering north of 60 to be in economic development, but it doesn't hurt.

On the flip side, you may be white, a man and over 60, but that doesn't make you PMS. You earn your PMS stripes by:

• How you think.

• How you act.

Are you living in a community run by the PMS? Let's listen:

The PMS say, "We just need to attract new jobs."

Bull. **The next generation first picks a place to live and *then* looks for work.** Announcing that you have 250 new jobs does not import talent to your community, especially if your community is deemed "uncool" by the next generation.

Further, not all jobs are created equal. When I lived in Iowa, Governor Terry Branstad boasted that he "grew" Iowa's economy by 10,000 jobs. Sounds good, right? Well, most of those jobs were low-paying positions that attracted immigrants and the working poor, who in turn put tremendous pressure on Iowa's education and social service providers.

When school districts turned to Governor Branstad to help pay for ESL teachers, he pulled out empty pants pockets. No money there. He probably used it to lure those 10,000 jobs to Iowa.

The PMS say, "We just need to offer Very Big Companies multimillion-dollar tax breaks, and they'll locate here."

True. And look what happened:

> In 1998, the Kansas city of Manhattan and the state offered Sykes, a large call center company, a subsidy package of about $6.2 million based on its promise to create an estimated 432 jobs. From the city came a $2.6 million cash grant, free land, $500,000 for site improvements and property-tax reductions for five years. The state provided $550,000 from an "Economic Opportunity" fund, enterprise zone tax breaks worth nearly $1.8 million, and a project and training grant of $800,000.
>
> In June 2004, the remaining 256 workers lost their jobs when Sykes moved the work to Asia and Latin America. The Manhattan plant closed only six months after the enterprise zone tax breaks expired.[43]

Evidence shows that large tax breaks and incentives to lure jobs to your community end up as a form of corporate welfare.[44]

---

[43] www.corpwatch.org/article.php?id=12540, adapted from *The Great American Job Scam* by Greg LeRoy.

[44] Greg LeRoy, *The Great American Job Scam*.

Think about it for a second. If someone married you because of your money, people would gather in the parking lot of your wedding reception to place bets about how long the marriage would last. Well, the same is true in your community. If companies relocate to your community simply because you've offered the largest incentive package, they're not in it for love, honey.

All is not lost, though. There's a new generation of economic developers who get it. And they're kicking butt!

Austin, Texas, was a sleepy Texas college town in the 1980s. Then along came a bunch of economic development newbies who were too green to know they couldn't do something. And *whammo!* Austin is on everyone's "Cool Community" list.

It wasn't all that long ago that Denver, Colorado, was berated by the popular press as having "nowhere to go" as a city. Then along came a regional partnership of leaders who committed to marketing the region, not just its zip code.

Add a Mayor (Hickenlooper) who pulled the city out of the jaws of bankruptcy and whose next-generation political agenda includes adding high-speed rail (done) and ending homelessness. *Voila!* Another region on everyone's "Cool Community" list.

While Denver ranks as one of the best communities for small business, Mayor Hickenlooper is rated one of the five best mayors in the country.[45]

Nashville is also taking a new-economy approach to economic development.

> *My job in the coming years will not be to attract companies. One hundred percent of my job will be to attract talent.*
>
> —Janet Miller, Nashville Area Chamber of Commerce

These folks understand that **the next generation first picks a place to live, and then finds a job.**

---

[45] *Time Magazine*, April 18, 2006;
   www.time.com/time/press_releases/article/0,8599,1050348,00.html.

As we said in the opening chapter:

**Three out of four Americans under the age of 28 say that
a cool community is more important than a good job.**

Next generation economic developers know that if you want to attract the talent who'll work in your companies, become your civic leaders, donate to your charities, attend your arts and cultural events, you must have more than good jobs. You must have a city—a place, neighborhoods, and Stroll Districts—that captures their sensibilities, matches their values, and attracts and engages them.

An Open Letter to Economic Developers

Dear Economic Developers:

I know I come down hard on you in this chapter. My intention is not to honk you off; it's to provoke you to greater leadership. You see, the next generation is counting on you to build communities they'll want to call home in the future, not to reinvent the way things were.

I know it's not all your fault. After all, your performance is measured based on one thing: jobs. That was okay in the 1960s, because if you attracted the factory, you got the people, and the economy boomed.

But "jobs" are a crappy metric for a Knowledge Economy. You need to update how your performance is measured. Remember: The goals of economic development are to increase the incomes of *all people* in the region, which is supposed to result in *better* education and *better health*, more *sustainable economies* and increased environmental protection.[46]

Scored against these metrics, economic developers are failing. The next generation is growing up in communities with greater divides

---

[46] See these definitions in http://en.wikipedia.org/wiki/Economic_development.

between the rich and the poor, declining test scores in math and science, and infant-mortality and life-expectancy rates that are improving at a slower rate than the rest of the world.

It's a new century now, and the next generation is counting on you to build cool communities where they and their families can be engaged and enriched.

Jobs alone aren't going to attract them. You need to orchestrate a full-court press of economic and community development that includes educational leadership, environmental sensitivity, and a process for attracting and rewarding sustainable business practices.

If you can do that, you stand to leave a legacy—a destination that the next generation chooses to call "Home." I believe you can do it. The next generation needs you to do it.

Your community's coolness is a trump card in the race for talent. Your ability to attract and keep the *Live First* generation will determine if your companies stay in business, your arts organizations keep their doors open and your tax base remains stable.

The old rules of economic development don't work in a Knowledge Economy.

Truth #2: Cities are for people.

Not cars. Not interstates. Not parking lots. *Cities are for people—* a timeless truth as relevant to my dad's generation as it is to mine. The difference is, there will be fewer people to go around in the coming years, and the next generation sees and values cities differently than previous generations did.

To attract and retain the next generation of knowledge workers to your community, *you must see your city through their eyes.*

What are they looking for in your community?

Diversity.

Today's classrooms look more like the United Nations than *Leave It to Beaver.* At Kirkwood Community College (Cedar Rapids, IA), there are 27 countries represented in the student body. At U.S. colleges and universities, 30 percent of the student bodies are from outside the U.S.

The *Live First* generation is coming of age in classrooms rich with cultural, religious and ethnic diversity. The subtext they're absorbing is that great talent is not restricted to a certain gender, country of origin, religion or any other demographic label.

Talent just *is.* And the next generation's knowledge workers want to live and work near other smarties.

Companies recognize this. Corporate "diversity" programs aren't just feel-good initiatives cast forward by a "Make Love, Not War" generation. There's a bottom-line business dividend paid to companies that roll out the red carpet to all talent.

Take the Fortune 100 "Best Places to Work" list.[47] On the 2007 list, 70 of the best employers offered domestic partner benefits, up from 28 in 1998.[48] These CEOs don't care if their employees march in Gay Pride parades. They just want to engage and leverage all talent at work.

The next generation's appetite for diversity spills over into their lifestyles and community choices. If they can choose to live in San Francisco, whose website is offered in six different languages,[49] and eat authentic Chinese food in Chinatown, why not?

How diverse is your community? Do your city councils, nonprofit boards and "Leaders of the Year" look more like Ward Cleaver or the United Nations? Is your community run by the same 100 people who make all the decision and serve in all the leadership posts?

If you're not diversifying, you're dying.

---

[47] Learn more about the 100 "Best Places to Work" at
http://money.cnn.com/magazines/fortune/bestcompanies/2007/snapshots/1.html.

[48] www.sas.com/news/preleases/011007/news1.html.

[49] www.ci.sf.ca.us/.

Diversify or Die:
The City of 100 and the Irish Potato Famine

What does the Irish Potato Famine have to do with diversity in your community? Allow me to connect the dots.

In 2004, we worked in a community where we'd been tasked to identify strategies to attract and engage young professionals. During a meet-and-greet with the region's leaders, I realized that all of them seemed to be close friends. It felt sort of like high school. I commented on this to one of my tablemates.

"Oh, yeah," he said, "This is really a city of a hundred people. The same people are on all our boards."

Our research in their community had drawn a similar conclusion: Many of the young professionals we'd surveyed were transplants to the region, who reported having a hard time getting involved in the community.

So I asked my tablemate, "How can a young professional penetrate this group of a hundred?"

"They just have to bully their way in," he said.

Hmmm . . . not exactly an inclusive, engaging strategy. Certainly, "bullying" works for some transplants, those with Teflon skin and unshakeable confidence. But in most communities, "townies" have supreme advantages: namely, the best Rolodexes and the most historical knowledge of how things work.

Which leads me to the Irish Potato Famine, attributed in part to the fact that there were so few different genetic strains of potatoes in the country. This, unfortunately, made it easier for one virus to infect and kill much of the crop.

What happens in regions where a "town of 100" dominates?

In science, it's called lack of genetic diversity. And it's tied to extinction.

If our communities' leaders are not cross-pollinating outside their "town of 100"—those same familiar faces whose conversations can degenerate into groupthink—their communities may also face extinction.

Third Spaces.

Another indicator of a Cool Community is Third Spaces.

A Third Space is not home (the "first space") or work (the "second space.") A third space is an in-between space. It may be a coffee house, a martini bar or a bistro. Third Spaces are generally busy and locally owned. Many have funky restrooms.

Fido in Nashville. Alterra in Milwaukee. A Third Space is your local "it" place where ideas—and often caffeine—collide. Birthplace of the start-up. Ground zero for the mind-blowing creative alliance. A place where pink hair and gray hair are equally welcome. And that's the rub.

Third Spaces are "equalizers,"[50] places where people of all economic and demographic backgrounds rub shoulders . . . and share the lone decanter of half-and-half.

Third Spaces are important to young talent and critical to communities. In the safety of Third Spaces, members of the next generation plot their next career moves and dish about what's cool in their communities or bad about their bosses.

If taverns were the meeting places of Thomas Jefferson and front porches the meeting places of the Cleavers, Third Spaces are the places for talent in the Knowledge Economy.

Stroll Districts.

When you have a high concentration of Third Spaces, all within a couple of blocks, you just might be looking at a Stroll District.

Stroll Districts are people-friendly areas where:

- You can park once and spend the rest of your afternoon walking from store to store and experience to experience.

- Retail shops—both locally owned and boutique chains—attract discretionary dollars.

- There's a human scale to the sidewalks and storefronts, making them accessible to window-shoppers and passers-by.

- People eat and drink "al fresco" in the open air.

---

[50] I first heard Pat Algiers (formerly with Kahler Slater and then the City of Milwaukee's Department of City Development) use this phrase to describe Third Spaces.

- People languish at cafés and on park benches.

- Cars brake for pedestrians.

- Both "townies" and visitors congregate.

Stroll Districts are important—like Third Spaces—because they bring a level of equalization to cities. On the sidewalks of the Stroll District, you're reminded that you share the community with others. You brush against (and sometimes smell) all kinds of people.

Stroll Districts make an important contribution to the local economy. The concentration of shops in a single district shakes more change out of purses, and locally owned shops create a greater economic impact by keeping dollars in their local economy.

Want to take a walk in a Stroll District? Visit State Street in Madison, WI; Pearl Street in Boulder, CO; Brady Street in Milwaukee, WI; or "Eat Street" in Minneapolis, MN.

Density.

Although I might sound to you like a new urbanist, please hear me out. *Density is important because it allows more opportunities for people to connect with each other.*

You might be thinking, *But the next generation doesn't care about connecting with others. They isolate themselves with their technology. Why, they don't even walk down the hall to tell me something at work! They send me an email.*

Guilty as charged. Which is why density is so important.

Density shakes us loose from our narrow-casted lives and lurches us into the human cauldron of culture and society at the heart of the nongenetically modified event we call *life*.

In *High Tech, High Touch*, John Naisbitt wondered how our addiction to technology would impact our ability to relate to each other. Today, kids hide their parents' BlackBerrys to command some much-needed attention.

Population density may be the key to more connected lives . . . to a renewed sense of the public good.

Lie: The next generation is lazy and apathetic

This is an insidious lie, uttered by people who lack the mental muscle to get out of their own heads and see the world through the lens of the next generation.

The truth is, the next generation is aching to be engaged. But since they're unwilling—or unable—to do it in traditional ways, they're written off as apathetic soloists by the folks who hold the reigns in most communities.

Here's a short list of some of our most celebrated civic organizations, with their founding years:

Elks Club, 1868

Rotary, 1905

Moose Lodge, 1906

Boys and Girls Club, 1906

Kiwanis, 1915

Lions Club, 1917

League of Women Voters, 1920

In his book, *Bowling Alone*, Robert Putnam charts the decline of each of these institutions, which all happen to parallel to the decline— that is, dying—of the folks who founded them, the Lost Generation (b. 1883-1900).

Putnam's book spews gobs of additional evidence to back up his thesis that our stock of *Social Capital*—the very fabric of our connections with each other—has plummeted, impoverishing our lives and communities. Putnam's stats are impressive: we sign fewer petitions, belong to fewer organizations, are less familiar with our neighbors, meet with friends less frequently and even socialize with our families less often.[51]

But that's not what I've been seeing on the front lines with the next generation.

Yes, Kiwanis and Rotary clubs are aging and dying. But cast your eye to some less traditional, more contemporary trends and a different story emerges.

---

[51] Interested in more of Professor Putnam's data? Check out www.bowlingalone.org.

Truth is, the next generation doesn't join Rotary, and most of us don't know the words to "My Bonnie Lies Over the Ocean." But that doesn't mean Next Gen'ers don't have our own gig going. Today, young professionals are showing up, reaching out, and digging in through Young Professionals Organizations (YPOs).

YPOs are popping up across the United States like freckles on a redhead. The Washington, D.C., young pros boast over 50,000 members. Pittsburgh has several YP orgs. The Young Professionals Network of the Illinois Quad Cities grew from a goose egg to over 1,500 members in just four years.

What's happening here?

For a relatively small and mobile generation that craves connection and impact, YP networks quickly link young professionals to each other and to their communities. Despite the media's portrayal of the next generation as lazy slackers, YP networks tell a different story. **Young professionals aren't apathetic; they just make a difference in a different way.**

Young professionals are engineers, graphic designers, architects, city planners, Web-heads, entrepreneurs, nurses, teachers and nonprofiteers. They're the "knowledge workers" predicted in 1959. They're trained to be problem-solvers, and they're intent on making a difference in their communities.

YPOs aren't social clubs or singles' scenes. YPs organize around issues and don't wait to be asked to sit at the Big People's Table. YPs are tackling thorny community concerns like land redevelopment, the arts, integration, housing, and leadership.

Every year, I hang with over a hundred leaders of YP groups from across the United States at the annual YP Summit. Here's what I've learned about your community's next-generation leaders:

- YPs know how to command media attention. If these folks were your PR team, you would have your own reality TV show. Maybe even a breakfast cereal.

- YPs are honked off that many of their community leaders view YP networks as "cute, little social clubs." In these cities, YPs are going around the traditional power structure or infiltrating it. Generally, they excuse the establishment's stupidity by referring to it as "old and slow." They're not waiting to be asked. They're inventing new, faster ways to effect change.

- YPs are intent on making their communities more inclusive of all kinds of diversity. Young professionals don't care if you're gay, straight, black, yellow, purple, have tongue rings, tattoos, or a Kathy Griffin fetish. Tolerance is passé; inclusion is where it's at.

- YPs are measuring their success (income and expense ratios, perception changes, talent attraction, and retention indicators) to make their case about the importance of attracting and retaining talent to your community. Think *YPs with MBAs*.

Birmingham's *Catalyst, Young Professionals Network* of the Illinois-Quad Cities and PUMP are just a few of the emerging models designed to engage the next generation.[52] They're similar to Rotary or Kiwanis in that their members are committed to building better communities. But they're different, too. They're more open, agile, and inclusive. You don't have to be nominated to join one of these groups; you just show up. To find out about events, you don't need to attend meetings; you just need an email address. There's no special handshake. No pins. No waiting periods. No guilt. Just show up. Reach out. Dig in.

Communities that embrace their YP networks and leaders stand to gain big rewards in their quests to attract and retain our world's scarce supply of young talent. **You're three times more likely to retain young talent in your community if they feel their voices are heard and valued.**

So what are you doing to engage them? A key finding of our *Cool Communities* research is, **the more young talent are engaged in their community, the longer they plan to stay.**

In fact, there's a direct correlation between the talent who say they feel "involved" in their community and those who plan to stay five years, ten years, or for life.

How do you involve young talent in your community—and stem brain drain—when they may not yet have the cash, clout, or connections you need on your boards, committees, and task forces? It starts with your acknowledgment that involving young talent is a community-

---

[52] www.ypcommons.org has a directory of groups like these in cities across the country and world. YP Commons is a service of Next Generation Consulting.

sustainability strategy. If they don't fit into a current slot, change the slots or create new ones. If you don't engage them, they'll vote with their feet and move to communities where they can feel connected and engaged.

Old Town and New Town: A Tale of Two Cities

In 1962, "One hundred eleven Atlanta art patrons die[d] in a plane crash at Orly field in Paris." The victims were Atlanta Art Association members who had chartered a plane to hear their city's orchestra play in Paris.[53] They were Atlanta's leaders—judges, executives and old-money folks. They were The Establishment. The Bluebloods.

And then one day, they were all dead.

This is a tragedy. Period. But it does pose an interesting question: What would have happened to Atlanta if those folks hadn't died? Would the city have grown to its current status as one of America's best, most diverse cities? Would the Honorable Shirley Franklin be Atlanta's mayor?[54] Or would the city have languished beneath the weight of its established egos, fortunes, and notions of grandeur?

I don't know the answer, nor can I speculate. But as we work in cities, I often get a bird's-eye view of leadership structures that are clinging to the past. I see leaders whose best days are behind them, and cities that would benefit if a few new faces were invited to the table.

Let's call these places *Old Town*. In Old Town, YPs (young professionals) feel disenfranchised because the "old boys network" is still operative. In these communities, *Who's your daddy?* is too often more important than *What's your idea?* And that's a darn shame.

---

[53] www.rootsweb.com/~gafulton/atlantahistorystuff.html.

[54] Mayor Franklin was also named, along with Mayor Hickenlooper, on *Time Magazine's* "5 Best Mayors" list.

Old Town powerbrokers cling tightly to their past—to the ideas, people and institutions that delivered them to power. They cannot for a moment bring their sights to rest on the present. The present is frightening. It operates at a speed that blows their hair back.

In Old Town, who's-right-and-who's-wrong is easy to discern because there are only two sides to every story: the side of the powerbrokers (the correct side of the argument) and the side of everyone else. There is little honest intellectual debate in Old Town because new ideas are a threat to the systems that put and keep the Establishment in power.

In Old Town, YPs wonder, *Who has to die in this community before we can have a voice in our future?*

But there is a measure of revenge. Today, YPs don't have to stay in Old Town. They can take the express train to New Town, where ideas have value, where innovation and energy—not age—are measures of their capacity to contribute.

New Town has a vibe that asks for the best from all people and gives a sense that the city's brightest days are ahead of them, not behind them.

What would happen if all of your community leaders were killed in a plane crash? Your answer might tell you a lot about whether you live in Old Town or New Town.

Truth #3: Cool Communities work together and play to win

I recently attended a women's basketball game. The team I was rooting for rallied before halftime, then went on to lose the game by ten points.

As the players shuffled into the locker room after the final buzzer, I caught the coach and asked, "That full-court press in the third quarter killed you, didn't it?"

She responded, "We know how to beat a press. But we don't know how to win. We spend more time trying NOT to lose than playing to win."

She's right. The team I was cheering for played like winners until halftime. They controlled the ball, were aggressive, and congratulated each other after good plays. But when the pressure was turned up in the second half, they unraveled. They hung their heads when the opponent scored. Individual players tried to break the press with solo heroics— dribbling into a corner—instead of keeping their heads up and passing to teammates. They stopped talking to each other.

When the heat is turned up in your community, do you rally together and play to win, or do you get sullen and defensive, revert to your silos, stop communicating and start finger-pointing?

To compete in the Knowledge Economy, communities are going to have to think and behave regionally. Talent already does. YPs live in one community, work in another, go to weekend college in a third, and hold season tickets in a fourth. If your economic development initiatives are not structured similarly, you're already a step behind.

One of my great frustrations is when communities that are practically Twin Cities—because of their proximity, synergies, or shared talent pools—cannot get their act together to leverage their potential. They try individual heroics rather than coordinated teamwork. Chamber and economic development leaders pass it off as "territorialism" or "lack of shared vision." Fractioned communities act out of fear. They're trying NOT to lose, rather than playing to win. At the base of that fear is an unproductive *either/or, win/lose* mentality.

Here's what communities are afraid of:

- Leaders want to get re-elected or re-appointed. They feel they must identify an "enemy" to stir up the emotions—and the votes—of their constituents. The truth is, voters are mobilized by powerful and *positive* messages. It's how Reagan beat Carter in 1980 with the vision of the city on a hill.

- Community councils believe their neighbor's good news (announcements of new housing developments or a grant for an entrepreneurial incubator) means they've lost. The truth is that the *people* who populate those housing developments and workplaces behave regionally. So when your neighbor lands a new business, its employees may choose to live in your community. Who wins? You both do!

To compete in a Knowledge Economy, you need the best—the best people, the best ideas, the best strategy—from your entire region. You have to keep your heads up, pass the ball to each other, communicate . . . and play to win.

> "Once upon a time, there was a generation of talent who placed as much value on where they lived as where they worked. Asked to choose between 35 years of workaholism in return for predictable promotions, a nice parking spot (and a potential downsizing) or living in a diverse, progressive community with oodles of occupational options and a solid after-hours scene, today's young talent pick 'B,' thank you very much."
>
> *Hot Jobs-Cool Communities Report*

Since we rolled out our *Hot Jobs–Cool Community* report in 2001, we've talked with thousands of members of the next generation via Web surveys, focus groups, and interviews. They've told us what makes communities cool, and we've cross-indexed what they've said with hard statistics about where the next generation really does live.

We've assembled our findings into seven indexes—the lenses through which the *Live First* generation looks at your community: Vitality, Earning, Learning, Social Capital, Cost of Lifestyle, After Hours, and Around Town.

Taken together, the scores in these seven indexes form your Cool Community "handprint." The bigger your handprint, the cooler your community. Your handprint can also reveal blind spots you may not have considered before. A sample "handprint" follows in this chapter.

1. Vitality

How "well" is your community? The Vitality Index measures your local commitment to the physical environment—air and water quality, as well as green space—and includes factors like fruit and vegetable consumption, obesity, and life expectancy.

If you eavesdrop in communities with a high score in the Vitality Index, you hear the next generation boast:

- "I can ride my bike to work, even in the winter! The city plows the bike paths!"

- "You have to check out the farmers' markets and one of our Slow Food restaurants."

- "Curbside recycling? We have that."

- "This is a great place to enjoy the outdoors. There are parks everywhere!"

- "Yes, you can get vegetarian food here—or any kind of food, really."

Which communities earn a high *Vitality* score? Here are a few great examples:

- Nashville's Mayor Bill Purcell committed to putting every Nashvillian within a ten-minute walk of a public park, trail, or recreation area.

- Minneapolis recycles everything from metal to microfiber.

- Alexandria, Louisiana, is committed to recycling outreach and education.

- A year-round farmers' market like the one proposed in Cedar Rapids, IA, is more than a market; it's an experience. Think of Pike Place Market in Seattle or the newly reinvigorated Edmonton (Canada) City Market. People go just to go, not necessarily to shop.

2. Earning

In April 2001, *Time Magazine* reported that by the time they're 32, the next generation will have had nine jobs. When choosing a community, young talent aren't looking for the one company where they'll work the rest of their careers. They're looking for a breadth and depth of occupational options.

They're also looking for communities that are friendly to start-ups. The U.S. Small Business Administration estimates that **as many as four out of five new businesses are started by women, X'ers, and minorities**.

To achieve a high score in the Earning Index, we listen for and measure factors like:

- What is your commitment to entrepreneurs and start-up companies?

- How many patents have been received in your community in the last three years?

- How diverse is your local economy? If one company fails, are there others who can pick up the laid-off employees?

- Must your young professionals move to another community to fulfill their career aspirations, or does your economy offer a breath and depth of options?

Cities like Columbus, Ohio—which has a range of public- and private-sector employers—score well in the Earning Index.

3. Learning

Today's young talent are lifelong learners. Over 60 percent of them have had some training beyond high school, and they intend to continue their education—formally and informally—for life. **This index measures the key indicators that define education, continuing education, and re-education opportunities.**

Let's say you're Cambridge, Massachusetts. Harvard University, Harvard Law School, and Harvard Medical School call you home. Does this mean you'll get a good score on the next generation Communities Learning Index? Not necessarily.

The next generation is interested in learning beyond terminal degrees (MBAs, JDs, and other graduate degrees). Today's young people want to learn Pilates and Plato, salsa dancing and Spanish. In other words, enrichment . . . not necessarily advancement.

To determine your community's Learning score, we measure attributes such as:

- Percentage of graduates from high school, two-year and four-year colleges, and Ph.D. programs.

- Number of colleges and tech schools.

In focus groups we listen for voices like:

- "We have several great bookstores here."

- "I took a cooking and wine-appreciation class last month."

- "My creative writing club meets on Thursdays."

- "Yoga classes are offered at all skill levels."

- "The library here is incredible."

So, how do communities earn a high *Learning* score? Here are three who did:

- **Milwaukee, Wisconsin:** Restaurateurs link up to offer gourmet cooking classes (www.grandgourmetwi.com). How about a top-shelf gourmet cooking party for your friends? A tuxedo-attired chocolatier?

- **Portland, Oregon:** Powell's City of Books has an entire shelf dedicated to local and visiting authors (www.powells.com). Libraries and bookstores of any size can play a critical role in promoting local authors and cultivating a culture of shared learning through book and writing clubs.

- **Racine County, Wisconsin:** Head of Economic Development Gordy Kacala organizes several mountain-biking experiences annually. He just plain loves to teach his favorite sport to riders of all levels. Got gloves? A helmet? Let's go!

These three *Live First* communities offer a breadth of learning experiences and educational options for talent of all ages. When it comes to the next generation, it's definitely about enrichment, not necessarily advancement.

4. Social Capital [55]

It takes many voices to create the chorus we call a Cool Community. This index tallies a community's commitment to diversity and its citizens' social, professional, and political engagement in community life.

"Social Capital" is a concept that has been around for decades, but the phrase was actually coined and popularized by economist she-ro Jane Jacobs in her 1961 book, *The Death and Life of Great American Cities*. Although it has been resurrected in Robert Putnam's recent *Bowling Alone*, Jacobs originally used "Social Capital" to describe the deep value of diverse urban neighborhoods.

---

[55] Jane Jacobs coined the phrase "Social Capital" in *The Death and Life of Great American Cities*, 1961.

At NGC, we use "Social Capital" to identify both the diversity within your community and your citizens' levels of engagement.

"Social Capital" is an important metric to the next generation. For an increasing number of educated Americans, diversity—of cultures, ethnicities, and thinking—is a valuable part of community life. In other words, some communities cultivate diversity because it attracts and engages enrichment-seeking young talent.

For a primer on next generation Communities with high scores in the *Social Capital* index, visit large university towns like Madison, WI, or San Diego, CA. In these communities, the university's presence engenders both diversity—of professors and students—and a heightened sense of community activism.

5. Cost of Lifestyle

This index is simple to understand. How much cabbage do young people need to keep a roof over their heads, clothes on their backs, and fuel in their tanks? Once we've determined that, we compare it to their wages.

Since young talent are in the early years of their earning potential, affordability in a given community is key. The Cost of Lifestyle Index includes all the variables in the national Cost of Living Index, which includes housing, food and transportation, plus a few others. **Midwestern, Midsouth, and rural areas are hidden gems for young professionals.**

Heads Up!
(directed especially to Midwestern communities):

When attracting young talent to your community, it's not enough to say, "Our cost of living is lower." If your wages are also lower—which they usually are—it's a wash. You need to sell your communities based on a combination of the seven indexes (Vitality, Earning, Learning, Social Capital, Cost of Lifestyle, After Hours, and Around Town).

To assess your community's score in the Cost of Lifestyle Index, start by asking yourself these three questions:

1. Can a young professional buy a respectable starter home for $150,000 or less in our community? The number of homes purchased by Americans under 25 has doubled since 1990. Housing affordability matters.

2. On a night out, how much will a young professional spend on dinner at a hip restaurant, tickets to a show, parking, and drinks?

3. How does the average salary of an entry-level computer programmer, customer service rep, educator, graphic designer, retail employee, accountant, or attorney compare to the national average?

6. After Hours

Adulthood is being pushed back for young professionals. In Europe, there are 46 million single-person households. Marriages in the United States happen at an average age of 27 for men and 25 for women; 42 percent of our workforce is unmarried.[56]

Naturally, the next generation is looking for ways to connect to their peers.

The After Hours Index identifies the cool "stuff" to do after five. Young talent want places to go, things to do, and ways to recharge their batteries. Communities with a diverse array of After Hours spots score well with young talent.

Communities with high scores in the After Hours Index hear their young talent say things like:

- "Let's meet at the new martini bar after work."

- "Want to go to *Symphony with a Twist* on Thursday?"

- "I want to catch that new local band this weekend."

- "You can go out dancing every weekend if you want!"

---

[56] "Top Ten Trends," Now and Next, www.nowandnext.com.

7. Around Town

This index identifies the key indicators of accessibility, or the physical connectedness of a community. How easy is it to get to where you want to go? How close are you to an urban hub? **Young talent may be perfectly happy to live in smaller communities if they have easy access to the shopping, eating, and entertainment options available in bigger metros.**

To achieve a high score in the Around Town Index, ask yourself the following four questions:

1. How close are we to the next big metropolitan area?
2. Is there reliable highway, train, or airport connectivity to larger metros?
3. Is my community friendly to runners, bikers, bladers, and pedestrians?
4. Do we have rush hours or rush minutes in our community?

Speaking of rush hours, consider this from the Texas Transportation Institute, the largest university-affiliated (Texas A&M) transportation research agency in the United States:

> *"At a time when fuel is increasingly costly, traffic jams are wasting 2.3 billion gallons of gas every year."*

The next generation cares deeply about our environment. They care—a lot—about wasting gas, wasting time, and wasting energy—theirs, in particular.

TTI's research, published annually in its *Urban Mobility Report* is useful, in that it details traffic-congestion delays in the nation's busiest cities. Once only a big-city problem (for example, in Los Angeles, San Diego, Houston, Chicago, and Washington, D.C.), traffic congestion is an ever-worsening problem in much smaller cities, too.

Here's the point: No matter where you live, traffic congestion is a big deal. And, as TTI says, "When you're sitting in traffic and trying to get somewhere, it's the only deal." (www.tti.tamu.edu, January 2007).

The 7 Indexes at Work

Once we tally your scores in each of the seven indexes, we plot them on a spider diagram and call it a "handprint" (see Raleigh-Durham's handprint below). As of this book's publishing date, a score of 4 is the national average. The larger the handprint, the "cooler" the community.

The value of an X'ercise like measuring your handprint is to see your community as the next generation sees it. In business, if you were rolling out a new product for the next generation, you would examine your product from their perspective.

Measuring your handprint is simply being customer-centric... from a city's point of view.

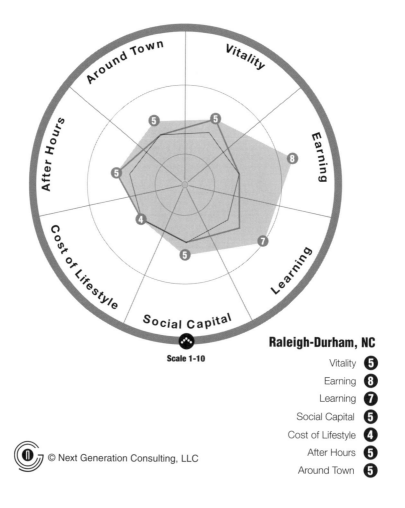

Scale 1-10

Raleigh-Durham, NC

Vitality	**5**
Earning	**8**
Learning	**7**
Social Capital	**5**
Cost of Lifestyle	**4**
After Hours	**5**
Around Town	**5**

© Next Generation Consulting, LLC

2.3 FREQUENTLY ASKED QUESTIONS ABOUT COOL COMMUNITIES

Q: Can small communities be cool?

A: Yup. The key is to determine your positioning. Muscatine, IA, can never be New York City. But it does have three Fortune 500 companies that call it home, and it's located on the beautiful Mississippi River. Most communities, large or small, have assets that they can leverage to attract the right talent to their communities. Please read "Is Bigger Better?" on page 73.

Q: Do we have to excel in all areas of our handprint to attract and keep the next generation?

A: Nope. I've seen communities earn a good score in only one or two indexes and leverage the heck out of it, and with great effect. Alternatively, there are some cities that have great handprints, but all their momentum is heading south. Your handprint is really just a snapshot to help you see yourself through the lens of the next generation so that you can take appropriate, strategic steps to attract and keep them. A great handprint does not guarantee talent-magnet status. Neither does a weak handprint indicate that you'll suck swamp water for the rest of your days.

Q: How do we convince our community leaders and politicians to invest in Cool Community strategies?

A: It depends on those you're trying to convince. I try to understand what motivates leaders and who influences them. For example, if your mayor is a real estate wheeler-dealer, then you use that angle to get her attention (*e.g.*, appeal to her desire to reuse a blighted area and reinvent it as a live-work hub for YPs).

If your leaders are entrepreneurial, appeal to their need to be the first or the best. If you don't have the leader's ear, figure out who does and provide them with your research and recommendations. A single comment from a trusted advisor can affect a leader's position more quickly than a hundred letters to the editor. Be patient and persistent.

If all else fails, sometimes you can appeal to a leader's desire to leave a legacy, or to have their children and grandchildren move home. Ask, "Why don't your kids live here? What would it take to bring 'em back?" I've seen County Commissioners over 80 years old who refer to their grandchildren when casting a vote for entertainment districts, al fresco dining ordinances, and workforce housing for teachers. They're rock stars in my book.

Q: *I'm a young professional. Who has to die before I get a seat at the table?*

A: Good question. I hope you read *A Tale of Two Cities* in the previous chapter, because I wrote that for you.

I feel your pain. In some communities, the Townies have a strong hold, and they view all Transplants as a threat. It's not malicious (usually). It's an auto-response; they feel a strong wind of change, and their instincts tell them to hunker down and turn away. It's very off-putting to transplants, that's for sure.

Let me ask, why do you *want* a seat at the table? If it's because you really love your city, and want to make a positive impact, don't give up. Make a list of the leaders you respect most and ask for their insight on how you can make your community better. What boards would they recommend? Where are the organizations and leaders who want engaged, new blood?

If you don't love your city, and you simply want to be engaged, maybe you're living in the wrong community. I live in Madison, Wisconsin, and most people are not from here. I've found it very open to Transplants, welcoming, and an easy city to live in.

Penelope Trunk, author of *The Brazen Careerist*, has written an excellent article on how to choose a city that's right for you. I RIFF on her article in "Anatomy of a Relocation" on page 69. (FYI: Penelope lives in Madison, too.)

If you're committed to your city but you still can't get a seat at the table, maybe other people feel the same way, and you could all build your own table together? Visit www.ypcommons.org to find out how.

Anatomy of a Relocation

Pick a place to live and then find a job, or ask your company to let you take your job with you. That's the *Live First, Work Second* ethic in action. Penelope Trunk outed a few Next Gen'ers who have made exactly that decision in her *Boston Globe* article, "Let Quality of Life Be Your Guide." Trunk dissected the seven key decisions to a successful relocation.

Here are my favorites from her list, along with some supporting points from NGC's *Cool Community* research. If you're a relocator, I recommend that you read Trunk's entire article.[57] If you're a Cool Community leader, jump-start a discussion with your peers about how to recraft your community's marketing messages around these issues.

• *Pick a city with career flexibility.* No one expects to work 25 years in a row for the same company. The next gen will have multiple careers and potentially dozens of jobs. But if they can have all of those experiences in a single city, then whammo: You have a stable tax base.

• *Choose a city where your median income won't leave you in the poorhouse.* There are a gob of new books hitting the shelves about happiness. Experts says that keeping up with the Joneses is a condition of chronic unhappiness. So if you pick a city, or a neighborhood, where you feel poorer than those around you, you're bound to be unhappy. If you'd like to learn more about the economics of happiness, the BBC has an excellent video series. Check out *Good Stuff* for the BBC link.

• *More choices do not always mean a "cooler" city.* It's true: Choice can be overwhelming. Just because the "Let's Go" section of your

---

[57] http://bostonworks.boston.com/news/articles/2006/11/12/letqualityoflifebeyourbeacon/.

newspaper is brimming with options doesn't mean they're all good, or that they're the right ones for you. Consider what's happened with TV. We now have hundreds of channels, and there's still nothing on. More "After Hours" activities doesn't necessarily mean a higher quality of life. You can do only one thing at a time, anyway.

• Keep your commute short. Amen! Traffic sucks. Period. Research by Dr. Robert Putnam, author of *Bowling Alone*, shows that for every ten minutes spent in traffic, people decrease their civic participation by 10 percent. Want more Girl Scout troop leaders? Build live/work communities so people can walk to the office.

Q: What about the suburbs?

A: Suburbs are part of a region. You can't be a suburb to nowhere. It's in a suburb's best interest to promote and support the 'downtown' amenities—the Stroll Districts, arts and culture districts, and business centers—that make your suburb a possibility.

Q: If we reinvent our city for a Live First *generation, will we have to do it again for the next generation?*

A: Maybe. Community development is like the laundry. There's always more to do. Don't let this be your excuse for waiting 20 more years to establish and implement a plan.

Q: Retirees are the fastest-growing segment of the U.S. population. What about strategies to attract them?

A: NGC research indicates that empty-nest Boomers and young professionals often want the same things in Cool Communities: vibrant downtowns, locally owned bars and restaurants, population density and ways to plug into learning. Why not build communities that appeal to both segments?

Many real estate developers are building high-end loft and condo projects to appeal to empty-nest Baby Boomers whose kids are out of college and have big cash to spend. This is the free market at work, and developers are charging top dollar to maximize their profits. I studied economics. I get it.

But think ahead five years. What happens when only one kind of person can afford to live downtown? You create rings of suburbs that suck income and property taxes out of the central city. Eventually, companies move their campuses out of downtown to be closer to employees. This increases traffic congestion, causes pressure on the city's arts and cultural communities— who have to fight traffic to build an audience—and decreases people's willingness to engage civically.

Smart cities recognize that they need a housing mix. If you want young professionals to live downtown, you have to include housing that they can afford.

Q: *I have a daughter who moved away to a larger city. When she starts her family, I'd really like my grandchildren to be closer. What can I do?*

A. My dear friend, you have magical powers to bring her back. See the "Granny Effect" in the text that follows.

> **When a child is born, so is a grandmother.**
> — *Italian Proverb*

They grow up. They move away. They move back home. We call them "boomerangers"—the young, educated talent who are causing "brain drain" in communities like yours. Don't despair. When they leave, it might be temporary.

Lots of cities will be competing to attract young knowledge workers to their communities. What will be the killer app?

Grandmothers.

Let's put this to work. The average Next Gen'ers are in their late 20s when they're first married. Many of these are starter marriages, so add three years. By the time the next gen truly settles down and has children, they're in their early to mid 30s and jonesin' for better connections to their parents. And not just for the baby-sitting benefits. Many of them become authentically nostalgic and "come home" to raise their own families.

We call this the "Granny Effect."

How can you put the Granny Effect to work in your communities? One of the most powerful tools to attract young talent to your communities and companies is person-to-person, word-of-mouth marketing. Sure, talent talks to talent. But talent also talks to their parents. And despite what any kid might say about heeding his parents' advice, no one has the ear of the next generation like parents do. Just look at Mother's Day. It's still the busiest day of the year for florists and telephone service providers.

So, how can grandparents be viral marketers for your community?

You just have to figure out how to tap into Next Gen'ers longing to return home. Some next-generation community leaders are already doing it.

Here are three fine examples:

- Nebraska employers get involved with their communities' 10- and 15-year high school class reunions. They host bus tours to showcase what's new in the community. The goal? To reintroduce grads to the community and the employment options available.

- North Dakota's Governor John Hoeven frequently phones "expatriates" considering returning to the state.

- The *Cedar Rapids Gazette* offered a special pull-out feature in the newspaper. The entire section was filled with stories about the area's largest employers. Soon the newsroom was getting calls from anxious moms requesting additional copies. They wanted to wrap their kids' holiday presents in the newsprint to send the subliminal message to "Move back home."

Is Bigger Better?

In the wake of 9/11, and buoyed by advances in digital technology, many young, talented people are leaving super-metros to pursue work and life ventures in more remote areas of the country. *American Demographics* predicts that the rural Midwest—with abundant fresh water, hard workers and affordable lifestyles—will become one of the fastest-growing regions in the country.

The Rural Handprint
The Iowa Department of Economic Development invited Next Generation Consulting to work with six diverse Iowa communities to determine each area's "handprint" and collaborate with local leaders on strategies to attract and retain talent.

The Rural Advantage
Two rural Iowa communities—Muscatine (pop. 22,697) and Carroll (10,047)—had unique, positive results. Both communities outperformed the national average in several indexes.

> "Bigger is not always better. Rural communities frequently outrank larger metros because our process judges community amenities on a per capita basis, accommodating communities of all sizes."
>
> —Rebecca Ryan
> Next Generation Consulting

Challenges
Rural and small communities face several distinct challenges:

1. Young talent perceive fewer opportunities to lead in small, rural communities. To attract and retain young talent, next-generation communities must make a place at the table for young talent and purposefully invite them to join in decision-making. Young professionals' networks (see www.ypcommons.org for a directory) are one place to start.

2. Small towns must tell their story on the Web and be diligent about positioning themselves on "Best Small Towns" lists. The Web is the best tool to reach young talent, with costs to market online coming down every month. Engage tech entrepreneurs who've chosen your community or those who know it well, and ask them to in-kind their services in return for your referrals.

3. Entrepreneurship. Four out of five new businesses are started by Gen X'ers, women and minorities. How friendly is your community to start-up companies? Are small-business loans, high-speed Internet access and professional networking available and published?

2.4 11 THINGS YOU CAN DO TO BE COOL

In April 2004, I was presenting to a full house about building "Cool Communities" that would attract and keep the *Live First* generation. It was late in the afternoon. The cocktail reception was next. I was the only thing between 500 thirsty people and Happy Hour. But first, I had to take a few questions.

I answered two easy ones. Then came the bomb.

A man in his mid 40s stood up in the middle of the room and asked: "Rebecca, all this talk about Cool Communities . . . I have two teenagers who remind me every day how UNCOOL I am. How can I be more cool?"

The audience cracked up, but the guy was not laughing. He had a Cool Complex. I don't know if my response was right or not, but here's what I said:

"To be 'cool,' stay open, keep your thinking limber. Hang out with people who look, act, and smell different from you. If you're white, join the Urban League. If you're Protestant, celebrate the Seder or Kwaanza. Learn to sing *Feliz Navidad*. If you like jazz, go to a mosh pit. Take yourself on a date to the art center, or anyplace where you have to figure out where to park. Get out of your comfort zone. Have conversations with people who stretch and elevate your thinking."

When Peter Drucker died in November 2004 at the age of 95, he was one of the coolest men in the world because of his curiosity and wide-ranging interests. Did you know that he wrote two novels in addition to his dozens of management treatises?

Beyond that, it's proven that lifelong learning leads to longer life. So, stay curious. . . not just about the next generations, but about anything that tickles your brain.

If you're a parent reading this book and trying to wrap your head around this Live First *mindset,* remember that all teenagers will at some point decide that their parents are the most *uncool* people they've ever met. If your kids don't do this, they're not normal. Or you're not. But beyond that, there are ways to stay cool, which is just another way of saying *relevant, fresh,* and *limber.*

12 Ways to Be Cool

1. *Quit talking about it and do it: Start or join a Young Professionals Organization.* Visit our website for a start-up guide,[58] and plan to attend a YP Summit. (Social Capital)

2. *Stretch yourself.* If you're white, join the Hispanic Chamber of Commerce[59] or the Urban League.[60] (Social Capital)

3. *Invite a young professional to the decision-making table.* (Social Capital)

4. *Buy every single birthday, anniversary, holiday and "just because" gift or card from a local merchant or artist.* (Social Capital & After Hours)

5. *Have coffee, breakfast, or lunch at a funky Third Space.* (After Hours) Extra credit for going with someone who looks, smells, or thinks different from you. (Social Capital)

6. *Start looking at your community through the lens of the next generation.* Hint: Developers may love strip malls, but they're not on the *Cool Community* map for young talent. Parks, trails, and recreation areas are another matter. (Vitality)

---

[58] www.nextgenerationconsulting.com.

[59] You can find your local Hispanic Chamber here: http://www.ushcc.com/mem-direct.html.

[60] You can find the Urban League affiliate listing here: http://www.nul.org/affilatelisting.html.

7. *Develop a new scorecard for economic development that includes* Cool Community *metrics like SBA funding for small businesses, number of patents, Stroll Districts, and population density.* Be the catalyst for jump-starting a new conversation about economic and community development. (All Indexes)

8. *Get smart.* Put these books on your reading list: *The Death and Life of Great American Cities* (J. Jacobs); *Bobos in Paradise* (D. Brooks); *The Rise of the Creative Class* (R. Florida). You bookish, overachiever types can get a longer list in the *Good Stuff* section at the back of the book. (Learning)

9. *Tune in.* A lot is being broadcast and podcast about developing Cool Communities. Start here:

   www.smartcityradio.com/smartcityradio/ (Learning)

10. *Eat fresh.* Most communities have a farmers' market. Buying local is good for the economy and great for your health. Produce that's grown in your area has more vitamins and minerals because it stays on the vine longer, giving it the most time to develop all of its essential good stuff. (Vitality)

11. *Be people-powered.* Do you drive to work when you could walk or ride your bike? The next generation prefers communities that are multi-modal and pedestrian-friendly. Commuting by bike or on foot creates fewer CO_2 emissions and leads to a slimmer, fitter you. And that's just plain beautiful! (Vitality)

12. *Get creative.* Invent your own sampler platter of the arts. In the next six months, attend a music or theater performance, a visual arts event, a spoken-word event, and an "underground" arts event. This is good for the arts, of course, but it's also good for your brain. Being exposed to the creative economy enhances our mental muscles by exposing us to sights and experiences that are outside of our usual day-to-day lives. (After Hours & Social Capital)

Now . . . stay cool.

CHAPTER 3

ENGAGING THE *LIVE FIRST* GENERATION AT WORK

3.1 THE MEMO: EMPLOYEE LOYALTY IS DEAD
THE BLOG: EMPLOYEE ENGAGEMENT IS BORN

One December, I got a call from a bank president in Nebraska. It went something like this:

"Rebec-CA!" He sounded like a WWII drill sergeant.

"Sir?"

"Rebecca, I've got a big problem at my bank. We're going through a back-office conversion.[61] I need these Gen X'ers because they're the only ones who know how to program these computers. The project is running over time and over budget because they keep leaving before the job is done. They'll run down the road for ten cents more an hour!"

"Sir, how can I help?"

"I need you to come in here and give these Gen X'ers a pep talk!"

"A pep talk?"

"I need you to tell them why they should stay and finish this project!"

I was stunned. I'd never been asked to do something like this before. He thought the problem was the next generation, or ten cents more per hour. I had to think fast.

"Sir, I wonder if you'd be open to an idea . . . "

"Shoot!" Like I said, he sounded like a drill sergeant.

"Well, I'd like to talk to the Gen X'ers who left and hear from them," I said. "Then I'll come in and talk with you about what I've learned . . . and I'll talk with the Gen X'ers, too. I think we can get this figured out."

"Great. I'll have my girl Gladys get in touch with you."

Gladys was 63 years old. She was the General's executive assistant and was very helpful. I got the names and home telephone numbers of every Gen X'er who'd left. I started dialing.

---

[61] As I understand it, a "back-office conversion" means that the bank is upgrading all of its back-office functions so that, for example, customers can see their cancelled checks online, rather than having them mailed with their monthly statements.

I called the first guy. They were all guys, these digi-geek deserters.

"Hi. My name is Rebecca Ryan, and your previous employer is paying me to find out the real reason you left The Bank."

"For real?"

"Yup."

Silence.

I've learned to hold silence because if I wait long enough, the interviewee will usually gush. I call it the Oprah Effect.[62] My silence cracked this guy open like a nut.

He puked, "Dude, have you heard about *The Memo*?"

"Not yet. What's *The Memo*?"

"Awwww, man. We got this memo the Friday after Thanksgiving. It was a real buzz kill. Mandatory overtime, the works. It was such a crock, because the working conditions were already crummy. And *The Memo* made them worse. A whole bunch of us started looking for new jobs right away."

"Tell me about the working conditions."

"Ohmygosh . . . for starters, we worked in the *basement*. There was no sunlight at all. And none of us had keys to the building, so we had to work between 8 a.m. and 5 p.m. Believe me, those aren't cool office hours for any of us. It felt like being in lock-up or detention, or something."

"So, what was in *The Memo*?"

"For starters, it was issued the Friday after Thanksgiving, which was supposed to be a day *off*."

"Uh-huh . . . "

"And then there were all these new rules in it. You wouldn't even believe it."

He stopped talking, and I heard something in the background. "You know, I still have a copy of *The Memo* here. Do you want to see it?"

I got *The Memo* via fax a few minutes later. After five or six calls, it was clear that *The Memo* was a lightning rod for the exodus.

---

[62] The Oprah Effect: The overwhelming urge to tell your life story to a complete stranger on national television. Or, in this case, to an author of a book.

MEMO

DATE: November 26, 1999

TO: Back-Office Conversion Contractors

FROM: *Name Withheld*, VP-Operations

SUBJ: ***Effective Immediately***

As you know, our back-office conversion is running over time and over budget. In an effort to get this project back on track, the following changes will go into effect immediately:

Beginning next Saturday, there will be mandatory overtime. All contractors will work on Saturdays from 8 a.m. to 5 p.m. until the project is completed.

There will be no more eating or sleeping at your desks. I have asked our office administrator to make regular rounds in your department. Any persons sleeping will be awakened, and a note will be placed in their personnel files. Anyone eating at their desk will be asked to take their food and beverage to the first-floor break room, and a note will also be placed in their personnel files. This will be a "three strikes and you're out" policy. After three infractions, you will be terminated. This bank prides itself on a level of professionalism that is sorely lacking in your department.

Every other evening, our vending machines are checked and restocked. I have asked our distributor to withhold Mountain Dew until further notice. I have reviewed the contents of Mountain Dew and feel that the sugar and caffeine contents may have an adverse effect on the completion of our project. In addition, the empty cans in your department are a hazard, and I would like them thrown away immediately.

I know that if we pull together, we can make up some time and have this project completed by the first of next year. Thank you in advance for your cooperation. If you have any questions, please contact our office administrator.

The Memo was like kerosene on a match. Within days, the contractors started leaving and the bank was hemorrhaging talent at the precise moment the COO was trying to get the project back on track.

Anyone who works on personnel issues knows that every story has two sides. So let's run down both sides of this issue:

COO's Perspective	Contractors' Perspective
I'm responsible for an on-time, on-budget completion of the back-office conversion.	"We're only contractors" and have no loyalty to the bank or to the completion of the project. In fact, once the project is done, we'll be discarded because our services are no longer needed.
The project is behind schedule, and we need to make up time to keep our schedule.	First, you make me start at 8 and quit at 5, and now you want me to give you my Saturdays, too? Why don't you just give me a key to the basement and I'll work 12-hour days, noon to midnight Monday through Friday? Those are my peak work times anyway.
Eating and sleeping at your desk are unprofessional. No banker would be caught sleeping at his desk, and the break room is the space everyone uses for eating lunch.	No one sees us; you keep us locked in the basement! Plus, when we're in the 'zone' and the programming is coming fast, I don't want to leave my desk to eat or even pee! Finally, like I said before, 8 a.m. is not a good start time for me. I'm still sleepy. Why can't I start at noon and work 'til midnight?
The sugar and caffeine content in Mountain Dew is too high. It's leading to lack of focus and hyperactivity. And what's with the pyramids of empty cans?	Dude, you are SO out of touch! Mountain Dew keeps me focused and in the game, especially when I have to start at 8. What if I took away your Folgers? Plus it's fun to build stuff in the basement with the empty cans.

At the center of this issue—and hundreds more like it in American workplaces—is a difference of opinion about how to engage employees and what employees and employers expect from each other.

From the COO's perspective, his authority role and the bank's paycheck should be enough to engage his charges. It was for his generation: You did what you were told. You didn't ask questions. You fell in line. Left. Right. Left-Right-Left.

But consider that the COO also had—and has—job security. So long as he did what he was told, he had a job. And at the latter stages of his career, it's doubtful that he'll be dismissed.

Not so for the next generation. The COO's notion of employee loyalty was already on life support when they were born in the 1970s, 80s, and 90s. And it died soon after.

The August 25, 1985, headline in *The Boston Globe* read, "AT&T TO ELIMINATE 24,000 JOBS: CUTBACKS TO TRIM COSTS, BOOST PROFITS."[63] By the end of the 80s, GM, IBM, U.S. West, and others cut 3.4 million jobs in the United States.[64]

As the next generation was being born and growing up, employee loyalty died. Corporations killed it. It was called "downsizing," "rightsizing" or "re-engineering." Whatever its name, the massive layoffs of the 1980s and subsequent recession left a deep gash in America's security blanket.

After the layoffs, *both* parents headed back to work in order to make ends meet. The nuclear family exploded and, with it, the vestiges of employee loyalty and/or corporate paternity.

Gen X'ers and Millennials grew up learning to rely on themselves—not employers—for economic security.

Still, like the COO, many employers continue to *expect* employee loyalty. They keep the idea of loyalty on life support, pumping more dollars, benefits, and memos into its feeding tubes. They believe that if they pray long enough at its bedside, loyalty will begin breathing on its own again. This is a myth.

Employee loyalty is dead. May it rest in peace.

---

[63] Accessed at http://nl.newsbank.com.

[64] *Rekindling Commitment: How to Revitalize Yourself, Your Work, and Your Organization*; Dennis T. Jaffe, Cynthia D. Scott, and Glenn R. Tobe, 1994, Jossey-Bass, San Francisco, CA, p. 14.

The next generations have no delusions of job security or any financial security, really. More believe they will see a UFO than receive Social Security.[65]

So, the riddle for every COO, leader, manager. and businessowner becomes "How do I engage workers with a *Live First, Work Second* mindset?"

The answer? Throw away those memos. Start a blog.

Now, hold your horses. I'm not suggesting that you go off and start a blog today.[66] All I'm asking is that you consider the difference between memos and blogs:

	Memos	**Blogs**
Direction	Top down	Multi-directional
Purpose	Give direction, instruction or correction	Provoke a conversation or discussion
Point of View	Management's	Multiple; anyone can comment, start a new blog, dig or de.li.cious your post(s)
Tone	Bureaucratic	Ranges from friendly to outright anti-authoritarian
Implies	There's one right answer, and it belongs to the memo-writer	The group is smarter than the one

Memos are vestiges of my dad's top-down, command-and-control, Beetle Bailey management structure. If you think and act like a Memo-Head, you probably also believe that loyalty is something automatically granted by employees who are just grateful to have a job. But that's not the case for the *Live First, Work Second* generation.

---

[65] Bruce Tulgan, *The Manager's Pocket Guide to Generation X.*

[66] But if you really wanted to, you could go to Blogspot or Blogger to start one.

What's more, Memo-Heads could take a lot of pressure off themselves if they'd stop writing memos and start blogging. Memos infer that the writer has The Answer for everything, including how to engage employees at work. Memo-Heads believe that it's their job to figure out the secret sauce, cook it, and serve it up. WRONG.

If you want to know how to engage employees, **ask them**. They'll tell you! The next generation has come of age in an interconnected world. They're talking about you, your management style, and your company via I.M., text messaging and at vault.com. Why shouldn't they tell you?

So rather than sticking to your old-school, memo-writing ways, loosen up and have a conversation—or start a blog—with your next generation. Ask them what you can do to engage them at work, and you'll have a fighting chance of keeping them.

What Happens When You Ask Them?

Reznick Group is one of the fastest-growing CPA firms in the U.S. When the firm's leadership—all entrepreneurial, *A* types—saw the mixed results of their Next Generation Company™ survey,[67] they wanted to take action. So they asked over 80 of the firm's up-and-comers (most in their mid 20s) to determine what the firm should do to improve its ability to attract and retain talent.

In one morning, these Next Gen leaders brainstormed three dozen critical issues to address. After lunch, they whittled it down to six, formed study teams, and gave themselves four months to develop business cases and make recommendations to the partners. *And they did it all during tax season.*

Their recommendations ranged from *firing bad clients* to *alleviating Saturdays*. The partners are committed to taking action.[68]

---

[67] The Next Generation Company™ survey is a proprietary tool my team has created to help companies attract and retain young talent. Learn more at www.nextgenerationconsulting.com.

[68] www.ReznickGroup.com.

When you task the next generation with a stretch assignment that has real-world implications, stand back. They'll be more engaged. You'll start a different dialogue. You *will* retain them. Go ahead, think like a blogger.

3.2 WHAT DOES THE NEXT GENERATION WANT? AND OTHER INSIGHTS FROM THE SECRET DECODER RING

My firm is often hired to conduct employee-engagement surveys. This is a good first step to retain talent: Ask them what they value and how well they think your organization delivers.

In the survey results, we often break talent down by age, gender, married/partnered, etc. The intent is to tease out any differences between groups.

The results are often intriguing. While the *Live First, Work Second* generation does rank certain things like "life/work balance" as more important than their older counterparts do, the overarching stimuli that evoke greater engagement are generally similar among cohorts of all ages.

What am I saying? I'm saying that people are people. By introducing people-centered practices and perks in your organization, you'll retain not just the *Live First* generation; you'll more deeply engage all employees. This is consistent with a long line of management gurus from Peter Drucker to Jeffrey Pfeffer, who advise that you must engage employees' heads *and hearts* if you want to get the best from your people.

Further, in a Knowledge Economy, your ability to attract and keep smarties has a direct impact on your competitiveness. As Larry Bossidy writes in *Execution: The Discipline of Getting Things Done*, every organization needs three core processes:

- One for *budgeting and operations*
- One for *strategy*
- One for *people*

This chapter is about your people strategy and how to engage the *Live First, Work Second* generation.

Following are the top four things the next generation wants from work:[69] Control over their time, Straight-A Management, Training, and Opportunities for Growth. Here, too, are some of our favorite stories from the Management Hall of Shame.[70]

1. Control over their time.

Forget the time clock. Throw away the punch cards. The next generation's *Live First, Work Second* ethic clearly states that what they do after 5 is as important—if not more important—than what they do between 8 and 5. Having control over their time means that the *Live First* generation wants to have a say in how and when they work—or don't.

"Control over my time" is often referred to as "work/life balance" in corporations around the planet. I cringe at this label. Why? **Pay attention! This is the *Live First, Work Second* generation. Calling it "work/life balance" reverses the priorities!**

There are two other reasons that the term "work/life balance" and its attendant practices make me nuts.

Let's start with hypocrisy. Companies hand out laptops and BlackBerrys like drug dealers pedal crack. We're told that these tools give us greater control over our time. They allow us to work anytime, anyplace. They do. And we do. We now work anytime, anyplace... and our 4-year-olds are hiding our BlackBerrys at home so we pay attention to our kids. Spouses complain that their significant other checks email in bed . . . yes, sometimes during sex.

Laptops, CrackBerrys, and cell phones are not work/life balance amenities. Unchecked, they're causing greater imbalance . . . and the scales are tipping in the direction of work.

There's a second reason I shrivel when I hear "work/life balance." It has to do with my dad, Elmer, and the lesson of the Five Balls I learned before he died.

---

[69] Based on over 5,000 surveys and interviews conducted between 1998 and 2002.

[70] On April Fool's Day (NGC's anniversary), we used to run a contest for the most idiotic management faux pas committed against the next generation. We pulled out a few of the classics to reinforce our point of view. Names have been withheld to protect people from their (stupid) bosses.

Five Balls

(Originally published at www.nextgenerationconsulting.com by Rebecca Ryan on June 24, 2004)

If you're keeping track—and I know some of you do—you've noticed that my regular Thursday ezines have been, well, irregular. And some of you have tolerated last-minute juggling while I made room in my calendar to attend to my dad's illness. Well, Dad took his last walk earlier this month. In his last days, I learned a very valuable lesson— the Five Balls—from a turbo-cool hospice nurse named Kelly. Here's how it went down:

A few days before my dad passed away, I was grilling his nurse Kelly to learn EXACTLY when he would die. His death was imminent, but since I had already cancelled or rescheduled so much work, I didn't want this to be a false alarm. Kelly candidly but gently advised that it would be just a couple of days.

Then she looked straight into me and said:

"Rebecca, I'm going to share with you my philosophy of life. Each of us is given five balls. One is rubber and four are glass. The rubber ball is work. If you drop it, it will always bounce back. The other four glass balls are family, friends, health and integrity. If you drop them, they are shattered. They won't bounce back."

Ironically, I write to you in this moment as a person who derives much of her esteem from the rubber ball. I work hard, and I love it. Then something comes between you and that rubber ball. In my case, it was my dad's passing. When the rubber ball is taken out of play, what's left? How well do we manage our glass balls?

Even more, I realize that our family, health and friends often happen TO us. There's little we can do to change circumstances around a parent's death, a divorce, or a diagnosis of a life-changing disease. But *integrity* is what we bring to the event. We can control and manage our integrity.

When teabags are met with hot water, they don't break. They have integrity. Rather than contract, they expand . . . and release their full flavor.

Having Integrity—that fourth glass ball—means keeping our word, acting in alignment with our deepest-held principles, telling our truths, and doing our very best in each moment.

I made the right choice. I cancelled work. I stayed with my family—and my dad—while he drew his very last breath on this plane. And it was one of the sweetest, most life-affirming moments I've ever experienced.

And Kelly was right. Work bounced right back.

I wish you great success in valuing and managing ALL five of the balls you've been given.

The Case for Life/Work Balance

Studies dating back to the 1920s have consistently shown that overwork is not sustainable. Tired employees make more mistakes. They take more sick days. Sometimes, their overtired misbehavior brings legal action against your firm.

From writing bad code to losing your temper with a co-worker, the American workplace is pocked with the scars of imbalanced employees.

The next generation of latchkey kids isn't having it. They know that LIFE is the headline and WORK is a subcategory. Companies like Patagonia (Ventura, CA) and SAS Institute (Cary, NC) understand, and they are rewarded with—you're not going to believe this—loyalty.

Yvon Chouinard, founder of Patagonia, perfectly summarized his life/work ethos in the title of his book, *Let My People Go Surfing*.

Dr. James Goodnight, a Ph.D. in statistics and founder of SAS, makes the business case for SAS's life/work balance amenities, including on-site child care and work hours that end—strictly—at 4:30 p.m. each afternoon:

"Creativity is especially important to SAS because software is a product of the mind. As such, 95 percent of my assets drive out the gate every evening. It's my job to maintain a work environment that keeps those people coming back every morning. The creativity they bring to SAS is a competitive advantage for us."

Compare that to your company. At many firms I ask leaders, "What do you do after 5?"

They respond, "Work five more hours!" It's no wonder heart disease kills more businessmen on Monday mornings. We're a nation of imbalanced workaholics.

Yes, there is a place for laptops, cell phones, and BlackBerrys at companies that value life/work balance. And one of the favored positions of those tech tools must be "Off."

Don't call employees on their cell phones when you know they're on vacation. Don't ask their kids to take down messages for them at home. Don't withhold promotions from people who have lives outside of work. They're the role models for the next generation.

We must start to call these people-centered, life-affirming methods "Life-Work" practices. Life is made up of five balls. Work is only one of them . . . and it's the rubber ball at that.

Management Hall of Shame:
Keeping long, looooong hours

This isn't a story about my manager, but it is a true story about one of the managers on our leadership team. We have a president—who's going to retire any day—and four VPs who are all jockeying for his seat. It's almost comical. All the VPs work very late at night. Sometimes I think Al (the president) is going to hand the keys to the corner office to the guy who sleeps there first.

Anyway, one of the VPs, Tim, is the Golden Boy. Everyone hates him. His office is closest to Al's, and he's a total brown-noser. One week, I had to put in some long hours to finish a new product we were releasing. My computer kept crashing because it didn't have the RAM to process all the applications I needed to run to get this project done.

Well, Tim had the best computer of anyone on my floor, so I went down to his office to see if I could finish up on his PC. When I explained, he threw me the keys to his office and said, "Sure, just lock up when you leave. I'm going home early tonight." (It was 8:30 p.m.)

He hadn't logged off from his computer, and somehow—I can't even remember how I came across this—I saw all of his recent page views on his web browser. They were all on porn sites. I remember seeing this and slowly taking my hand off his mouse, and feeling totally gross sitting in his chair.

Then I totally started cracking up because I realized that all this was going on while we believed Tim was working late, and he was really just screwing around—literally—online.

---

2. Straight-A management

Why did you leave your last job? We've asked that question to thousands of Next Gen'ers, and if we had a nickel for every time they told us that their last manager was a yutz-idiot-asshole-egomaniac-powertripping-unfeeling-jackass-scumball-womanizing-hot-headed-freakshow-all-hat-and-no-cattle pompous dick, we'd be retired on the beaches of Belize.

Bad management is an epidemic in this country. I've often joked that if the only thing we do at NGC is shine the light on the high rates of crappy and incompetent management in this country, we will have served the next gen well.

Funny thing is, it's not a joke.

A Next Gen'er's manager is the single most important person in their work life. No one can make or break them, retain or repel them like their manager. No one.

But that's not how companies are run. Perhaps it's a hangover of command-and-control, do-what-you're-told dictators. Most of our companies are run from the corner office. And shit rolls downhill. So if there's money to be saved or egos to be salved, managers will not take the hit. Employees will.

Companies should be run more like baseball teams. When the New York Yankees are losing, the owner doesn't trade all the players. The owner fires the manager. The manager is responsible for orchestrating all their talent into a winning team.

We take the opposite approach at work. Take the example of the bank president from the beginning of this chapter. He didn't look to his CIO and ask, "What the hell are you doing to these people that they're all leaving?" Nope. The bank president called me and asked me to give his young employees *a pep talk*. He assumed the problem was with *them*, not with their Memo-Head manager.

Management Hall of Shame:
12 steps . . . out of the building

I worked for a drunk. I didn't realize it when I started. I'd just heard that he had a bad temper. One day, he stormed into my office ranting about some paperwork that I'd incorrectly filled out. I told him I was sorry. He got so angry that he punched a hole through my wall!

After he left, I fled to a co-worker's office. I was sure Jim had heard what happened. As I explained in a trembling voice, Jim hardly looked up. Finally, he said, "He's drunk. He gets like that. Get used to it."

"He's a drunk?!" I was incredulous. "Why doesn't someone tell him to sober up?"

"Because he's a good salesman," Jim said.

I gave my notice and was out of there two weeks later. It was a hard thing to do at first, because I didn't have a new job lined up. But it would've been harder to stay, knowing that the leaders just tolerated this kind of behavior.

If you want to increase retention of young talent, demand Straight A's[71]—Appreciation, Acceptance, Attention, Affection, and Allowance—from your managers and employees. Here's how it looks at Next Generation Companies®, places that are talent magnets for young workers:

• **Acceptance.** How do you work with people who are different than you are, and get your work teams to do the same? How do straight managers work with gay employees? How do agnostics deal with

---

[71] Adapted from *How to Be an Adult in Relationships*, David Richo.

Muslims? Great talent comes from all corners of this planet and from all different walks of life. A great manager will orchestrate all that talent —all those differences and similarities—into a cohesive, high-performing team. At Next Generation Companies®, managers blend acceptance with high expectations. You can dye your hair any color you want, let your tats hang out, or pursue bizarre after-hours delights, but if you screw up a project—or screw over a teammate—you're out. At Patagonia, for example, you're free to surf anytime, provided it doesn't negatively impact your teammates or your customers.

Management Hall of Shame:
Accepting a female soldier

I was the only woman on staff. Eventually, I asked my boss why he didn't include me in his management team briefings and why we seemed to have such a hard time communicating. He said, "When I picked my soldiers, you weren't one of them." This pigeonholed me and set up an uncomfortable me-versus-them with my staff and my boss for the next ten years.

• **Affection**. This is going to knock a few of you back on your Herman Millers. I believe that affection is not only appropriate at work, it's necessary. Now, before you militant sexual-harassment-in-the-workplace Wobbleheads start flaming, consider the data. Next Gen'ers want to feel that they're a part of something bigger. Teams matter. The next generation attended prom as a group; they expect a degree of affection—or at least affiliation—at work. For my dad's WW2 generation, it was the brotherhood of the bunker. Dad knew that the guy he'd been in boot camp with—the PFC who ate the same crappy chow he did—that guy was going to be at his side in the bunker, fighting the same war, and would cover his ass when the shit hit the fan. Dad might have called it something like "loyalty" or "fraternity." But in the end, it was affection in a very selfless form. C'mon, admit it: In the best places you've ever worked, you felt affection for your teammates and your clients... maybe even your boss.

- **Allowance**. Allowance is different from Acceptance. Acceptance relates to people as they are; *e.g.*, "Even though I would never pierce my eyebrow, I accept that you have." Allowance, on the other hand, gives people psychic latitude to become even better versions of who they are. For example, "I know you're a summer intern here, but I wonder what your aspirations are and how we could help support you in your dreams?" When you give allowance to co-workers, you support them taking training classes that don't tie directly to their jobs. You encourage them to talk about their professional aspirations, even if they want *your* job. Working in Next Generation Companies® is not for the weak-kneed, my friends. Allowance calls on us to let pigeons out of their holes, tellers out from behind their desks, and executives the space and time to rediscover their passion. For Allowance to flourish, it helps to shed 'job description' thinking. At Brazilian-based Semco, Ricardo Semler allows employees to write their own job descriptions, choose their hours, and decide their wages.[72] That's Allowance.

- **Appreciation**. All of us want appreciation: a high-five when we close a deal, a personal note from a supervisor acknowledging our overtime. A lot of employees complain that they don't get enough appreciation from their bosses. I empathize; the thank-you note is almost passé in today's society, and bosses should definitely write more of them. But I also ask, "When was the last time you pulled any of your bosses aside and told them how much you enjoyed your work or their leadership?" At Next Generation Companies®, appreciation flows abundantly in all directions.

Companies that want to grow in appreciation benefit from the theory of the dipper and the bucket.[73] Offering appreciative words to others is like adding to their bucket. And when you work in an environment where personal buckets are full, people give more of their time—and themselves—to their teams and their jobs.

- **Attention**. Energy follows attention. Think about an elementary classroom. If the teacher gives a lot of attention to students who are misbehaving, what happens? Right—more kids start acting out. The reverse is also true. At work, if managers invest their attention in high

---

[72] For an interview with Ricardo Semler, visit http://www.abc.net.au/7.30/content/2007/s1864738.htm.

[73] Read "How Full is Your Bucket," available at http://www.bucketbook.com/.

performers by giving them the best clients and the most promising opportunities, soon other employees start to behave like high performers because they, too, want their boss's attention and all those opportunities. Now think about your garden. Your vegetables grow towards the sun. It's called the heliotropic effect and it works in human systems, too. Think about your personal life. You gravitate towards people who give you energy and make you feel good . . . and away from weird, old Uncle Bob, who sucks the life right out of the room. At Next Generation Companies®, attention is showered on the people, ideas, and issues that are generative, positive, and life-giving.[74]

Management Hall of Shame:
The screamer

I work in State Corrections. I broke my foot at work and had been begging the doctor to release me. Doc wouldn't budge. So I finally went to work—outfitted in a plaster cast and crutches—to break it to the boss that it would be another week before the doctor would fit me with a walking cast and release me to light duty. He didn't believe that the doctor wouldn't release me. The boss began screaming "colorful metaphors" at me and ended with, "You can sit on your ass here as well as you can sit on your ass at home!" Of course, everyone within earshot heard this. His tirade lasted several minutes and was pretty typical of his management style. Thankfully, he moved on to another shift and retired a couple of years later.

---

[74] If you'd like to learn more about how to give attention to life-giving forces at work, we strongly recommend a book or a course on Appreciative Inquiry. We could go on and on about the power of this approach in companies, and we've done so on our website: www.nextgenerationconsulting.com.

Getting Straight A's—Acceptance, Affection, Allowance, Appreciation, and Attention—requires intention and daily discipline. Here's a little crib sheet to help keep you earning Straight A's.

	Straight-A Manager	Clueless C-Class Manager
Acceptance	• Supports employees who take time off from work for family or personal interests. • Understands that sometimes, stuff happens; *e.g.*, flat tires, sick kids. • Is openly tolerant of people with different religions, lifestyles, hairstyles, etc.	• Acts like employees who take personal time are committing acts of treason against the firm. • Treats everyday inconveniences as if they were intentionally designed to make his/her life hell. • Makes ignorant comments about people who don't share his or her preferences in religion, lifestyle or hairstyle.
Attention	• Takes time and a personal interest in the career development of associates. • Is available for meetings with staff about personal and professional issues.	• Abides by the "no news is good news" management dictum. • Manages from behind a closed door or *in absentia*.
Appreciation	• Says things like, "Thank you for working the weekend" and "This report is so much better because you took the extra time to do the graphics." • Hands out on-the-spot awards like gift certificates for performers who go above and beyond the call of duty.	Hosts an annual party or picnic as one grand, sweeping gesture of thanks, while avoiding most human contact at the office.
Allowance	• Asks employees about their professional aspirations and works to find ways to help them achieve their goals. • Is flexible, offering options such as telecommuting, part-time, or flex-time to employees experiencing major life changes (*e.g.*, parenthood).	• Has a "my way or the highway" demeanor. • "Outside the box" is a frightening place, one to be avoided at all costs.
Affection	Calls you by name. Remembers your birthday and/or work anniversary. Is a source of friendship, not just a manager.	Says things like, "If you want a friend at work, get a dog."

3. Training

Which of the following investments elicits the greatest return to
your organization?

A. Training employees

B. Upgrading technology

C. Firing bad managers

If you answered *C*, you're a person after my own heart.[75] However, the
correct answer is *A*. For every 1 percent increase in employee competence,
your organization gets $8,000+ of increased productivity.[76]

So why is the training budget the first to get sliced and diced when
times are tight? I think it's because most training is poorly conceived,
rarely measured, and often has faint—if any—ties to actual corporate
performance.

Still, cutting your training budget is like volunteering for a lobotomy
before math team tryouts. In our Knowledge Economy, the constant
upgrading of skills is key to competing.

**Beyond its impact on the bottom line, employee training
is one of the best tools you have to attract and keep
the next generation.**

Remember: This generation relies on itself—not on you—for job
security.

---

[75] I'm on a personal crusade to eradicate idiotic management; see my dedication at the front
of the book.

[76] Source: UW-Milwaukee Advanced Management Series, April 2002.

The next generation and sees training as critical to building their brand, staying smart, and unlocking the key to their—and your—economic futures.

Tom Peters wrote a cover story for *Fast Company* magazine in August 1997 with the headline "The Brand Called You."[77] That magazine cover remains one of the most popular of all time at FC, and it could be the manifesto for the *Live First, Work Second* generation.

In the article, Peters challenges readers to think of their features and benefits the same way brand managers do, then position themselves accordingly:

"Start by identifying the qualities or characteristics that make you distinctive from your competitors—or your colleagues. What have you done lately—this week—to make yourself stand out? What would your colleagues or your customers say is your greatest and clearest strength? Your most noteworthy (as in, worthy of note) personal trait?"

To build their brand—to stand out from their competitors and stand up through the winds of economic change—Next Gen'ers know that they must continually sharpen and refine—and sometimes retool—their skills to remain relevant in a Knowledge-Based Economy. They need the training and the tools to do their jobs well, and do them better than competitors.

Unfortunately, at most organizations 75 percent of all training investments are made at the management level and above, leaving mere quarters on the table for non-management, Next Gen employees. That's a poor investment if you want turned-on, top-shelf, turbo-productive talent.

4. Opportunities for growth

At FirstEnergy, co-op students and interns are immediately put on project teams, where they are expected to deliver real results for the company *immediately*. Why? Because the smarties on FirstEnergy's talent-management team know that if they want to retain them as employees, interns and co-ops need to hit the ground running and have immediate challenges and growth opportunities.

At too many organizations, stretch assignments are few and far between. I think there are three reasons for this:

---

[77] Read the article at http://www.fastcompany.com/online/10/brandyou.html.

1. Managers underestimate the next generation, have low expectations for their new charges, and often assign 'busywork': projects with little risk and little return.

2. Managers don't know how to structure and supervise stretch assignments.

3. Managers falsely believe that career advancement and career opportunities are the same thing. I've spoken to countless *Live First* employees whose bosses do not understand that they *don't want a promotion*; they just want more training or lateral experience.

At Next Generation Companies® all employees are expected to hit the ground running. Mentors, buddies, and managers are explicitly tasked with helping new hires understand their roles and their impact on clients and the company. Next Generation Companies® line up their training and career pathways around clearly stated skills and experiences demanded by each position. And they relentlessly make career coaching a fixture in all conversations between managers and employees.

And here's the thing: Not all Next Gen'ers want their manager's job. Some of them are perfectly happy to grow in place without needing a promotion or taking on greater responsibility.

I was recently talking to a fellow consultant who shared a typical story. She was coaching a CEO who was very concerned about retaining two of his top performers. The consultant suggested, "Rather than promote them and pay them $250,000 per year and expect 80 hours a week, why don't you offer them $125,000 for 40 hours?"

The CEO replied, "They'd never go for that!"

The consultant, who had inside information on the situation, countered, "I'm pretty sure they would."

"No," the CEO said dismissively. "No one at this firm passes up more money."

In our shop, I call this *first-person bias*. Sometimes, we can't see the world through anyone's eyes except our own. When the CEO in the previous example said that no one in his firm passes up more money, he was talking about himself. He couldn't understand how anyone else would take less money—even if it was for less time. Sadly, he didn't offer it because of his distorted first-person bias.

So there you have it: Deliver these four things to the *Live First* generation at work, and you will have the secret code to unlock their potential . . . and maybe even their loyalty:

1. Control over their time

2. Straight-A Management: Acceptance, Affection, Allowance, Appreciation, and Attention

3. Training

4. Opportunities for growth

3.3 THE FLAVOR OF THE SUNDAE STARTS AT THE TOP: THE STORY OF NOAH & BILL AND LEADERSHIP BLOOPERS

> "Senior executives are prone to believe that their organizational status confirms that they know more about the industry, customer needs, competitors, and how to compete than the people they manage. But what they know more about is, all too often, the past. Every manager must face a cold, hard fact: Intellectual capital depreciates."
>
> —CK Prahalad and Gary Hammel
> *Competing for the Future*

A lot is written about leadership. I think it's because many of us have a Savior Complex. We want a strong, charismatic leader to sweep us up, inspire us to greatness, and save us from ourselves. It's *so* Hollywood. And, like Hollywood, it's pure fantasy.

My thoughts on leadership are unfinished. I know only a few things about leadership, so I'll share a story instead.

Noah and Bill

I was at lunch the other week with two corporate and community leaders: Noah-the-Boat-Guy and Bill-the-Banker.

Noah is a 60-something bald man. He arrived at lunch in a silver Lincoln Town Car. He wore slacks, a sport coat, and a tie with little ships on it. Cute. He was unassuming and soft-spoken. I had to lean in to hear him talk.

Bill-the-Banker also arrived in a silver luxury sedan. Like Noah, Bill is also a 60-something bald man. He wore a beautiful pink, silk tie with his tailored, gray suit. *Here,* I thought, *is a banker with some personality.*

I learned during lunch that both Noah and Bill had built good careers, were invested in their community and, ironically, both had multiple bypass surgeries.

During lunch, Bill talked about the deep investments he's making to build a service culture at his bank. Noah talked about saving the family's ferry business from bankruptcy. At face value, I considered both of them true-blue leaders.

My visit to their community lasted only 18 more hours. During that time, I got a deeper look at each of their organizations. Bill's employees were cordial and friendly when he took me on a tour of their new offices. But they dodged their boss at an after-hours function, and talked about him when he was out of earshot. Late in the evening, under the influence of who knows how many adult beverages, one of Bill's employees confided that she leaves the office in tears several times a week. Despite the investments Bill is making in training and building a service culture, employee morale seemed to be shriveling.

I also met Noah's employees—most of whom were teenagers— when I boarded his ferry headed home the next morning. Noah's employees, dressed in polo shirts and khakis, ran a very tight ship. They were courteous. They kept things moving. They exuded confidence beyond their years as they skillfully helped passengers park cars, herd children, and assign cabins. Most impressive, when I boarded at 9 a.m. there was Noah—dressed in the same polo shirt and khakis as the other employees—welcoming passengers aboard, and hustling to help passengers and teammates. No one would've guessed he owned the company; he simply acted like the oldest deckhand.

Both Noah-the-Boat-Guy and Bill-the-Banker have their hearts in the right place. But their actions are building decidedly different cultures, followings, and legacies with the next generation.

Which of these leaders would you rather work with?

Of course, no one sets out to be a crappy leader. We have poor role models. We get rewarded for cutting costs, not instilling loyalty. Donald Trump shouts "You're fired" if you stick your neck out too far and don't make the numbers.

If you want to be considered a leader of the *Live First* generation, here's a short list of leadership bloopers to avoid at all costs:

Leadership Bloopers

1. ***Be duplicitous***. Write long, poetic paragraphs about the importance of talent in your company's annual report. Behind closed doors—where shareholders can't see you—berate your top performers in front of others. Give yourself an enormous bonus, and freeze wages for the rank and file.

2. ***Pass the buck***. Blame turnover, poor performance, and toilet-circling morale on forces outside your control.

3. ***Take credit***. Is the stock price up? Must be because you're so smart. Are shareholders happy? Bask in the limelight.

4. ***Embrace bureaucracy***. Make new hires wait two to four weeks to get their computer, password and phone system. Require four signatures for a roll of toilet paper; six signatures for expense reimbursements.

5. ***Underestimate employees***. Don't task them with difficult assignments or expect too much from them. After all, you're the only one who knows anything around here.

6. ***Keep underperforming ROAD (Retired on Active Duty) warriors***. Don't fix 'em, and for the love of God don't fire 'em. Consider promoting them so that they supervise Next Gen employees.

7. ***Close your door***. Keep it closed.

8. ***Never, ever tell people how they'll be evaluated***. Back it up by "forgetting" performance reviews.

9. ***Offer young talent zero opportunities for skill-building***. Withhold training.

10. ***Criticize an employee's tongue ring, hair color, and/or wardrobe***. Then hijack their ideas to the boardroom and take credit for them.

11. ***Respond to new ideas with stock phrases*** like, "That will never work," "We tried that ten years ago," or my personal favorite, "Who the hell do you think *you* are marching in here with an idea?"

IMPLICATIONS OF *LIVE FIRST, WORK SECOND*

> All the perplexities and distresses in America arise…from downright ignorance of the nature of coin, credit and circulation.
>
> — John Adams in a letter to Thomas Jefferson
>
> August 25, 1787

To say that the next generation's *Live First* ethic is subsidized in part by an ignorance of the nature of coin, credit, and circulation is an understatement. I know. I'm one of them. I, like many of my Gen X sisters and brothers, amassed too much credit card debt on top of my student loan debt and wound up filing for bankruptcy in my 20s.

If Gen X'ers subsidized a *Live First* lifestyle on credit, Millennials are doing it on their *parents'* dime. While X'ers were considered losers for moving back home after college, Millennials think it's savvy. In 2003, 61 percent of college graduates planned to move home after graduation. In 2004, 57 percent were homeward bound.[78]

According to Bob Schoeni, professor of economics and public policy at the University of Michigan, "The percentage of 26-year-olds living with their parents has nearly doubled since 1970, from 11 percent to 20 percent."

Forget dot-com millionaires. Next Gen'ers are bordering on broke and bankrupt. Savings levels among the next generation are dangerously low, while debt levels continue to climb. Call it financial illiteracy.

Investors Business Daily found that the next generation either didn't know how much they'd saved or had saved less than $10,000 for retirement.[79]

And about that college education that's supposed to guarantee you a fat salary? Think again. "Recent college graduates owe 85 percent

---

[78] According to surveys conducted by MonsterTrak.com in March 2004 and May 2003.

[79] Dan Moreau, *Investors Business Daily*, May 2001.

more in student loans than their counterparts of a decade ago," says the Center for Economic and Policy Research.

In *Time*'s poll, 66 percent of those surveyed owed more than $10,000 when they graduated. Five percent owed more than $100,000."[80] Fannie Mae reports that the average college loan debt is $19,500.

"You need a college degree now just to be where blue-collar people the same age were 20 or 30 years ago. It's not that twixters don't want to become adults; they just can't afford to," quips James Cote, a sociologist at the University of Western Ontario.

Financial illiteracy among the Next Gen is rampant. It took me a bankruptcy to figure out how a mutual fund works and to calculate compounding interest, which most Next Gen'ers can't yet do.

American Value$

Over half of Gen X women recently reported that they're more likely to buy 30 pairs of shoes than save for retirement.[81] While this may seem financially immature, consider it in light of America's overall consumer culture. It is anticipated that more people this year will file for bankruptcy than will graduate from college, and more Americans will file for bankruptcy than for divorce.[82]

Like disease, conspicuous consumption will take its largest toll on the financially young and immature. Without credit histories or earning histories, high levels of debt coupled with intellectual immaturity make the next generation particularly susceptible to lives riddled with financial potholes.

It's time for straight talk to young people on finances. Otherwise, their standards of living will not only be lower than their parents' but our financial industries—housing, banking, and credit—will be so loosely strung together on poor financial insight as to render them extremely fragile.

---

[80] Lev Grossman, "They Just Won't Grow Up," *Time Magazine*, January 24, 2005, p. 45.

[81] Sutra Foundation and Oppenheimer Funds Study, 2001.

[82] John Annaloro, "Education As a Weapon Against Bad Debts and Fraud," *Seattle Business Journal*, May 13, 2005 (www.bizjournals.com/seattle/stories/2005/05/16/editorial4.html).

Suze Orman's *The Money Book for the Young, Fabulous & Broke,* Beth Kobliner's *Get a Financial Life,* and Eric Tyson's *Personal Finance for Dummies* give honest, "get real" approaches to getting out of debt, saving, and investing.

I believe in the *Live First, Work Second* ethic. But, from my perch, there are only two paths to sustain it:

1. Next Gen'ers will extend cash, coin, and especially credit to fund their lives.

OR

2. The next generation will scale their lives to fit their economic realities.

After my bankruptcy, I made a very conscious choice to teach myself all I could about money, finance, and its stewardship. I was *not* going to repeat the same mistakes again. Along the way, I learned that leading a true *Live First, Work Second* life requires a deeply conscious choice to live within your means. That way, work truly becomes an option.

For most Americans, this requires a major overhaul on how we think and what we allow ourselves to be exposed to. Marketers today know more about how to lure us into mindless spending than ever before, and credit is far too easy to get and abuse. No wonder we're ringing up unprecedented debt levels.

This leads not only to financial bankruptcy, but also to a numbing of our senses. Have you ever suffered stimulation overload at a mall? Have you ever had to just turn off the TV for a reason you couldn't explain? By the time a five-year-old child goes to kindergarten, she's already seen 125,000 ads. And that number will be higher by the time you pass this book along to a friend.

That level of marketing stimuli renders our want-versus-need meter useless. My brother Ron is an excellent example. He eats enormous dinners, sometimes to the point of stomach upset. But when the McDonalds ad comes on after the 10 o'clock news, he suddenly decides he's hungry. Obviously, Ron isn't really hungry; great marketing just makes him think he is.

To truly *Live First,* we must not pad our reality with material goods. We must be in touch with the things that naturally give us energy; things that rarely cost much at all. I'm hopeful.

While writing this book, I received many stories from people of all generations who are *Living First, Working Second.* David and Margo Knight left the Washington D.C. Beltway (and its attendant high-pressure, high-paying jobs) to live more simply in Brunswick, Maine. Then there are Michelle and Doug Racich. They planned for years so they could move their family to Northport, Michigan, where Doug could pursue art and Michelle, shiatsu.

There's a reason that *Real Simple* was the most successful magazine launch of the last several years. Perhaps Americans really are ready to *Live First* in the most natural, Waldenesque interpretation of the ethic.

May you always have *enough*. Stay cool and keep it simple. Take time to **Live First.**

And for crying out loud, if you like this book and found yourself talking back to it, please lend your voice to our online *Live First, Work Second* discussion at www.livefirstworksecond.com.

GOOD STUFF

Books and Multimedia

Unless noted, all of these resources are available through this book's website: www.livefirstworksecond.com.

Bobos in Paradise: The New Upper Class and How They Got There
David Brooks

Turning to One Another
Margaret Wheatley

The World is Flat
Thomas Friedman

Three Billion New Capitalists: The Great Shift of Wealth and Power to the East
Clyde Prestowitz

Execution: The Discipline of Getting Things Done
Larry Bossidy

The Great American Job Scam: Corporate Tax Dodging and the Myth of Job Creation
Greg LeRoy

Funky Business: Talent Makes Capital Dance
Jonas Ridderstrale & Kjell Nordstrom

Generations: The History of America's Future, 1584 to 2069
Neil Howe and William Strauss

Millennials Rising
Neil Howe & William Strauss

Snobbery: The American Version
Joseph Epstein

The Circle of Simplicity: Return to the Good Life
Cecile Andrews

The Death and Life of Great American Cities
Jane Jacobs

The Fourth Turning
Neil Howe & William Strauss

The Rise of the Creative Class
Richard Florida

"Negotiating Rent with Your Adult Children"
*Boomerang Nation: How to Survive Living with Your Parents . . .
the Second Time Around*
Elina Furman

What You Are Is Where You Were When—Again (video)
Morris Massey
Available at www.enterprisemedia.com

Affluenza and *Escape from Affluenza* (videos)
PBS Affiliate KCTS
Available at http://www.pbs.org/kcts/affluenza/

Supplement to Chapter 2: How'd We Get Here?

A side-by-side comparison of the four generations in contemporary U.S. society:

Silent Generation
b. 1925-1942

What shaped them: The Great Depression, Franklin Delano Roosevelt, World War II, Pearl Harbor, D-Day

Advanced technology: Automobile, telephone, black-and-white TV

At work: May be risk-averse; have a "by-the-book" mentality; value financial security, organization and authority; won't call in to work when their hair hurts; punctual

Icons: Ginger Rogers & Fred Astaire, Clark Gable, Frank Sinatra, Dean Martin, Babe Ruth, Shirley Temple, Hank Aaron, Joe Lewis, Roy Rogers & Dale Evans

Notes:
This generation is patriotic, perhaps because many were first- or second-generation Americans, or because they and their families fought in world wars. They have a strong sense of "Americanism" and they respect authority.

Baby Boomers
b. 1943-1960

What shaped them: Vietnam War, Woodstock, touchdown on the moon, ERA, the Pill, Watergate, President Kennedy's assassination, Martin Luther King, Haight-Ashbury

Advanced technology: Mainframe computers, color TV, cordless phones, PDAs

At Work: Prefer consensus to hierarchy, first generation of "workaholics," currently navigating the meaning of *work/life balance.*

Icons: Pope John Paul II, Mother Teresa, Warren Buffet, Walt Disney, Elvis, the Beatles, Simon & Garfunkel, the Beach Boys, Donald Trump, Dick Clark, Patty Duke, Ann Bancroft, Bette Davis, Robert Redford, Jack Nicholson, Paul Newman, Vince Lombardi, Bart Starr

Notes:
Many Baby Boomers were thrown off their career ladders during the massive layoffs of the mid 80s and have been bandied between mergers and acquisitions ever since. Because of this, Boomers may feel a general sense of dis-ease with risk, but believe they must "innovate or die." This generation values being "forever young" and will create new demand for cosmetic surgery, nonessential medications and youthful experiences.

Generation X
b. 1961-1981

What shaped them: Missing children on milk cartons, cable TV, mid-80s recession, computers in classrooms, space shuttle Challenger explosion, Iraq war

Advanced technology: *Star Wars*, the Internet, laptops, the Mac, Atari™, CDs, DVDs, surround sound, cell phones, instant messaging

At work: Unafraid to change employers; have a healthy disdain for hierarchy; want a "fun" workplace where they can learn new skills, build their Rolodexes, and enhance their portfolios.

Icons: Jeff Bezos, Bill Gates, Madonna, Michael Dell, Steve Jobs, Tiger Woods, Brett Favre, Barry Bonds

Notes:
This is America's first generation of latchkey kids. They have been self-sufficient from an early age, they are skeptical of institutions and they're savvy with media, information and technology. Gen X'ers are comfortable with change and are constantly seeking new opportunities to advance their skills.

Millennials
b. 1982-2002

What shaped them: President Clinton/Monica Lewinsky scandal, 9/11, Columbine school shootings, Nintendo and Sega, MTV, reality TV

Advanced technology: MySpace, YouTube, TiVo, iPods. BlackBerrys, WiFi, Bluetooth, Xboxes, Gameboys, plasma TVs, satellite radio

At work: Still too early to tell, but seem to favor information, communication and a democratic work atmosphere; want their ideas to be heard

Icons: Michelle Wie, Britney Spears, Jessica Simpson, Gwen Stefani, Eminem, Justin Timberlake, Usher

Notes:
Highest goal is to be *smart*; learned conflict-negotiation skills in elementary school and may use their communication skills at work. Despite the media's portrayal of them, Millennials have lower rates of violence, drug use, sexual activity and abortion than the previous two generations.

Meet Generation X

"Gen X'ers are lazy, disloyal, slackers." That's what the media says. I've even heard a county commissioner in Alabama say it. Maybe you agree. Unfortunately, much of the media's portrayal of Generation X is negative.

Certain things about Generation X drive some people nuts. Here's a short list of those "things":

1. Gen X'ers are a bullet-point generation; they don't read anything longer than a page.

2. They're *so* entitled! They feel like they should always get the next promotion, even if they've been on the job for only a short time.

3. They don't understand the value of chain of command.

4. Their manners are terrible. They don't say *please* or *thank you*.

5. They've never met an ironing board.

Which of these characterizations match your experience or expectations of Gen X? Some people—namely, Baby Boomers—find it therapeutic to scream, "YES! That drives me crazy about them, too!"

Traditionalists, on the other hand, might prefer more of a Bingo approach. In other words, when the numbers on the list match their opinions of Gen X'ers, they mark the matching numbers and . . . BINGO! Traditionalists win; Gen X'ers lose.

To this, a few Gen X'ers I know (okay, me) have something to say:

• The amount of information tripled overnight as we were coming of age. We grew up answering voicemails, emails, snail mail, pages and IMs. Bullet points are simply a coping mechanism. Besides, if you can't say it in a page . . . .

• If you deserve the job, you should get it regardless of seniority.

• The Chain of Command melted when the Cold War did.

• Thank you for pointing out that I sometimes forget my manners. I'm sorry. Please forgive me. I will try to do better.

• And about the ironing board . . . if I could afford a dry-cleaning service for everything, I'd use it. As it is, I'm trying to pay off my college loans before my kids start college.

All bitterness aside, I contend that much of the world has been misled. Generation X isn't nearly as bad as the media leads us to believe.

Gen X'ers are now out of college—well, except for that one guy who's been going continuously since 1988—and turning the corner from their early to their mid careers. Some have launched successful businesses. Others are managing people older than they are. Gen X'ers are starting families, putting down roots and taking leadership positions in our communities, albeit with priorities different from their parents'.

Like all generations, Gen X had defining moments that shaped them and permanently colored the lenses through which they see the world. To understand them, it's important to understand their unique perspective.

Generation X: The Four S's

SKEPTICAL. Gen X'ers came of age as American institutions were crumbling. The Iran-Contra scandal, declining U.S. scores in math and science, the Challenger explosion, corporate downsizing, unemployment, high divorce rates, razorblades in Halloween candy, and missing children were headlines as Gen X'ers grew up.

The result? A generation of Americans who don't talk to strangers and have little faith in institutions, especially employers. In other words, Gen X'ers are skeptical. They have a difficult time trusting others, they are obsessively self-reliant, and they don't see themselves as "joiners" of traditional organizations.

SAAVY. Gen X'ers were raised on a steady diet of technology and information. The first video game, Pong, came along during this generation's formative years. Soon, Atari and a bevy of other video games, electronics and computers became part of their lives. Network television expanded to Cablevision, which exposed them to millions of megabytes of electronic stimuli available 24 hours a day.

This generation has no recall of the olden days, when all three networks went gray at 11 p.m. to the sounds of our national anthem. They can't imagine life without the Internet, voice mail, email, cell phones, PDAS, and iPods.

Gen X'ers adapted to information overload and learned to manage it. They use technology and other resources to sift through gobs of information and make informed decisions. They're info- and tech-savvy, able to manage scads of data from multiple sources with ease. Gen X'ers are the first generation of multi-taskers.

SELF-RELIANT. By some estimates, 40 percent of Gen X'ers were raised in single-parent households. This is America's first generation of latchkey kids. With so much unsupervised time, Gen X'ers learned how to set the VCR, set the table, and set the agenda for what they wanted from dad on weekend visits.

This generation is highly self-sufficient. During the dot-bomb collapse, Gen X'ers took the massive layoffs in stride. Silicon Valley bars hosted *pink slip* parties. X'ers declared themselves in transition, went on retreats to Nepal and regrouped. Members of the latchkey generation know how to take care of themselves.

SWIFT (SPEEDY). Gen X'ers like fast computers, quick turnaround time, and instant access. As consumers, they do research, apply for insurance and comparison-shop electronically, preferring to search on-line than to wait *in* line.

Gen X'ers do face-to-face banking less than twice per year. Why? It's not convenient. And convenience is the name of the game.

In the second grade, Mrs. Abel taught us a trick to remember the spelling of *friends*: "Every friend has an *end*," she'd cluck.

In 2004, the last episode of NBC's *Friends* aired. When the show started in 1994, it centered on six 20-somethings facing life and love in New York City. When *Friends* ended, Ross, Monica, Phoebe, Chandler, Rachel and Joey are 30-somethings with more grown-up concerns; namely, spouses, children and settling down.

Many Gen X'ers matured along with the cast of this NBC sitcom. But to them, *Friends* was more than a popular show; it was an explanation and an exploration of what it meant to come of age in the 1990s.

If you want to understand Gen X, *Friends* is a good place to start.

There's a common misperception that successive generations follow the behavioral and attitudinal trajectory of the previous generation. In other words, whatever you're like is what your kids will be like. If this were true, Baby Boomers would never have protested the Vietnam War or, for that matter, questioned authority. Gen X'ers would not have job-hopped and Millennials would not be such amazing team players.

Bottom Line: Generations don't "follow" each other.

Meet the Millennials

That brings us to the Mighty Millennials. To prove that generations don't simply follow the behavioral cues of their predecessors, compare the next generations in the hyperbolic chart below:

Gen X'ers (b. 1961-1981)	Millennials (b. 1982-2002)
A latchkey generation, left alone to raise themselves.	A doted-on generation, born to parents who bought minivans and proudly posted "Baby on Board" placards on their windows.
Felt it was a sign of failure to move back in with their parents after college.	Feel moving back in with their parents is financially savvy; 77 percent say they value a good relationship with their parents.
Skeptical of authority.	Schooled in "Zero Tolerance" with a healthy respect for authority. Drug use, violence, and teenage pregnancy are declining.
Sometimes called "Slackers" for their perceived ambivalence toward ambition.	Value being smart.
Rely on themselves for job security. Often start their own businesses.	Value team experience and group achievement.

Managing the Millennials

Gen X'ers are independently minded and rely on themselves for job security. Not so the Millennials. They rank getting along with others, working well on a team, and getting along with members of different racial and ethnic groups "extremely important" skills for career success.[83]

Although there aren't yet enough of them in the workplace to make concrete management recommendations, we know enough about their upbringing to offer several considerations for employers.

Millennials will bring a unique generational perspective to the office. Raised in families that valued their ideas—and sometimes

---

[83] Drexel University *Futures Poll*, reported by Alison Wellner in *Training Magazine*, February 1999, p. 48.

catered to their wants—Millennials will expect similar consideration at work. At home, Millennials have been consulted on everything from where to go on vacation to which DVD player to buy. Often, their votes were decisive. Parents invested hundreds of weekends carting their Millennial wrestlers, acrobats, and club volleyballers to competitions.

Where Gen X'ers prefer "hands-off" management and tend to be entrepreneurial, Millennials need face time with managers and can be nurtured into loyal staffers.

Millennials will also bring intense technical, team, and communication skills to work. The World Wide Web didn't go mainstream until after 1990, smack in the middle of Millennials' birth years. Even the most technically illiterate Millennial has more computer training than today's average Joe CEO.

> Sarah is 8 and has been on the computer *for nearly 4 years.* She can program American Doll characters to address her on screen and download Spice Girls songs from one of her favorite websites. In addition to playing speaking, math and science games, she uses her computer to make personalized birthday and holiday cards for her friends and family.
>
> She has her own email address on her mom's computer and recently exchanged email addresses with a new friend while on vacation in Florida. In school she regularly communicates via email with a "key pal" living in Mexico. Meanwhile, she's learned how to research the Internet for a class assignment on white-tailed deer, and an elementary school publication has recently offered her a CD on basic programming.[84]

Health Concerns

Millennials' technical savvy comes at a cost. Weaned on a steady diet of computers and video games, children's technology-induced headaches, disorientation, and repetitive motion disorders have earned the term "Nintendonitis" in the medical community.

---

[84] Joan Throckmorton, *Direct*, May 1, 1999.

Seventy percent of American families own a video game player, and 33 percent of American children have these players in their rooms.[85] Because they started so young, Millennials may be predispositioned to repetitive stress injuries like carpal tunnel syndrome. Employers should ensure that they are in compliance with OSHA's standards for ergonomically functional workspaces.

Then there's the issue of the "TV dinner." In a typical week, Millennials spend about 20 hours watching television.[86] Households with high television use consume more caffeine, red meat, salt, and snacks. They consume fewer fruits and vegetables. Couple a sedentary lifestyle with a poor diet and *voila!* Obesity.

Among many pediatricians, obesity is the number one health concern for Millennials. For employers and managers, a heavier workforce could spell more—and more expensive—health insurance and Workers' Compensation claims, along with more time away from work. Next Generation workplaces invest early in preventative wellness programs.

If obesity is the number one health concern for Millennials, stress-related illness is second. Imagine fourth-graders throwing up before a band concert because they're scared they won't remember their music, or class valedictorians drinking bottles of the pink stuff to calm their stomach before finals. The pressure is on and the Millennials are feeling it. Frank Megorski, publisher of *Love Those Millennials* newsletter, says the drive for success at earlier ages has left kids stressed out. "They fear they won't achieve the high expectations society demands of them."[87]

---

[85] *Kaiser Family Foundation Report*, 1999, Shelly Jarenski in *Outpost Exchange*, February 2001, p. 16.

[86] *Kaiser Family Foundation Report*, p. 23.

[87] *Kiplinger's Personal Finance Magazine*, July 1999, p. 20.

Millennials: Their Own Four S's:

SMART. Millennials know they will have multiple careers in their lifetime, so rather than set their sights on a singular goal, they instead say they value being smart.

SPENDERS. When *American Demographics* was still a growing concern, they published an article that stated the average (self-reported) allowance Millennials receive each week is $68. (If you're a parent of a Millennial, you may want to take this fact along to your annual review when you ask for a higher wage.) Because of their size—they're on course to be an even larger generation than the Boomers—their spending power will be formidable.

SOCIALLY CONSCIOUS. Maybe it's because many high schools now require service-learning credits to graduate, but more likely because Millennials are some of the biggest-hearted people alive today. Maybe that's why Canadians call Millennials the "Sunshine Generation."

STRESSED. You can't run down the halls of a college sorority house without bumping into a sister taking Prozac, Zoloft, Paxil, or Wellbutrin. Millennials' anxiety and stress levels are mounting, due in large part to their overscheduled, high-expectation lifestyles. Millennials average 70 hours a week with school and extracurricular activities, and it comes at a price.

> *The object of adolescence is to figure out who they are. They don't have any time to sit down and figure out who they are. They are getting so fragmented, so compartmentalized, that they don't see how it all fits together.*
>
> —Sam Hestorff, Youth Minister
> Bayshore Baptist Church, Tampa, FL

Millennials approach *Live First* differently than Gen X'ers do. First, they have a more euphemistic mindset. They see their work as an end to a means; for instance, making the world a better place. Millennials are increasingly interested in public service occupations, nonprofit work, and volunteering.

A second contributing factor to Millennials' *Live First* mindset is having been raised in a society of uber-consumption. *You don't have to work to buy TiVo. You can charge it. Live first, Baby!*

This consumption characteristic explains a lot of Millennial behavior. In *Why White Kids Love Hip Hop: Wangstas, Wiggers, Wannabes, and the New Reality of Race in America*, author Bakari Kitwana suggests that one of the reasons white kids gravitate to Hip Hop is because it's a brand they can buy, wear, and belong to. All American kids—regardless of race—are raised in our consumer-crazed society.

To the end, **consumption** may unite us far more than race ever divided us.